LA TERRE
AVSTRALE
CONNVE:
C'EST A DIRE,

LA DESCRIPTION
de ce pays inconnu jusqu'ici,
de ses mœurs & de ses
coûtumes.

PAR MR SADEVR,

*Avec les avantures qui le conduisirent en
ce Continent, & les particularitez du
sejour qu'il y fit durant trente-cinq ans
& plus, & de son retour.*

Reduites & mises en lumiere par les
soins & la conduite de G. de F.

A VANNES,
Par IAQVES VERNEVIL ruë
S. Gilles 1676.

Title page of original edition (Geneva, 1676)

The Southern Land, Known

Utopianism and Communitarianism
Lyman Tower Sargent and Gregory Claeys
Series Editors

The
Southern
Land,
Known

Gabriel de Foigny

Translated and edited by
David Fausett

SYRACUSE UNIVERSITY PRESS

Copyright © 1993 by Syracuse University Press
Syracuse, New York 13244-5160

All Rights Reserved

First Edition 1993
93 94 95 96 97 98 99   6 5 4 3 2 1

David Fausett was born in New Zealand in 1950 and has studied there and in the United States and Europe. His doctoral work on semiotics and literature at the Ecole des Hautes Etudes en Sciences Sociales, Paris, was completed in 1988 and forms the basis of this book.

Library of Congress Cataloging-in-Publication Data
Foigny, Gabriel de, ca. 1630–1692.
    [Terre australe connue.   English]
    The southern land, known / Gabriel de Foigny ; translated and
edited by David Fausett.
      p.   cm.—(Utopianism and communitarianism)
    Includes bibliographical references and index.
    ISBN 0-8156-2571-5 (c1)
    1. Voyages, Imaginary.   I. Fausett, David.   II. Title.
III. Series.
G560.F65   1992
910.4—dc20   92-16909

Contents

Contents

Maps

Preface

This utopia is set in the legendary southern continent, Terra Australis Incognita, an enigma that by Foigny's time had begun to yield its secrets but would be finally dispelled only with the voyages of Cook one hundred years later. Early utopias exploited the incompleteness of geographical knowledge by offering fictive descriptions of such regions that were symbolic, rather than empirical, accounts of other worlds. As alternative models of communal life, they had a critical bearing on the writer's own society. Such works rose in popularity in the late seventeenth century, and that of Foigny is a classic among them, combining a thorough critique of social and religious ideologies with a lively story.

It reveals much about that age and about the use of utopias to explore social theory. A mixture of history, baroque fantasy, and allegory, it was long neglected but has over the past two decades been appreciated for its bold themes, tight composition, historical relevance, and colorful biographical background. Its oblivion owed partly to its eclipse by a bowdlerized edition published at the time of Foigny's death and partly to traditional ideas of what utopian literature was about. These ideas are undergoing major revision, which has been influenced not least by insights reached in the interpretation of this work.

The first English translation of the original text is presented here in the hope that it will be of value both to specialists and to students of literature or the history of ideas generally. The texts used or consulted include three modern French editions, copies of the original edition in the Bibliothèque Nationale, New York Public Library, Pattee Library (Pennsylvania State University), and Newberry Library, and of the abridged edition and its English translation of 1693 (the only translation hitherto made). I am grateful to the many in these institutions and elsewhere whose support, moral and material, has furthered my work on Foigny.

A text of this vintage always resists authentic translation; not only its words, but a whole world of thought must be rendered. That of Foigny is, in addition, often loose in style or typography and occasionally obscure in meaning. I have rendered his text in modern English, for several reasons: first, because a version exists that, although thematically unsatisfactory, is in the authentic English of 1693; second, because the raciness of the narrative could be lost in a translation that seemed stilted or convoluted; and third, because this might distract attention from the complex ideas in the work.

Similarly, I provide supporting information to facilitate a nonspecialist reading; but I do not deal exhaustively with the work's historical and critical background, which would itself fill a volume. I have imposed a normal paragraph structure where, as in certain vital dialogues, Foigny lets his run on at length and cuts the ideas at issue into inappropriate units; and I have added parentheses or quotation marks to clarify a confused sense. I have, in general, aimed to preserve the spirit of Foigny's foibles without compromising readability and to translate his ideas rather than merely his words.

With this aim too, my introduction moves from a traditional history of the author, the book, and the general background to a more personal analysis, focusing on Foigny's handling of the utopian device—his use of realism and narrative structure to order the ideas he presents and to take or imply a position on them. In this way I try to correlate the many facets of this complex work; that link, however, in no way pretends to be a final one that could chain Foigny to a definitive reading.

Mülheim-Ruhr, Germany   David Fausett
July 1992

Translator's Introduction

Gabriel de Foigny created *La Terre Australe connue* in Geneva in 1676 out of a life of turmoil. His only work of consequence, its career was to be marked (like his own) by denigration. It never achieved the reputation, for example, of More's *Utopia* or Swift's *Gulliver's Travels* yet was a worthy successor to the former and a forerunner of the latter. Like More and Swift, Foigny discusses perennial problems: the differences between cultures, religions, the primitive and the civilized, or nature and culture, and how to achieve harmony through education or politics. He even deals with some, such as gender relations, that have become widespread issues only in modern times.

Foigny's creation is an example of the "classical" utopias that were common before the rise of the modern social-planning variety. They were usually coupled with well-developed narratives—imaginary voyages to little-known parts of the world—and usually also characterized by a tone of ambivalence: the intention was not so much to illustrate in practice certain goals the author believed in as to speculate on the validity of any alternative social models or on the nature of society in general.

This sceptical, even conservative, approach linked the utopia to accounts of primitive societies rather than to political theory in a modern (especially revolutionary) sense. Such works reveal much of what earlier ages thought about society, both at home and as found in the New World. In relation to the ethnographic and geographic knowledge of the day, they represented, paradoxically, a form of realism. This aspect is central to *The Southern Land, Known* (and similar works of the period) and, together with a strong autobiographical element, forms the basis for an analysis of the work.

Foigny plays on the early belief in the existence of Terra Australis Incognita, a vast continent extending from the South Pole to the limits of the known world. It arose with the cosmological ideas of ancient Greece and was enhanced by tales and legends from other sources. From the sixteenth century the Portuguese and Spanish and, later, the Dutch began to sail the southern oceans; but because their voyages were usually veiled in secrecy, the legend lived on and even gained new significance for writers of utopias. For them, the continent not only represented a concrete, or even an epistemological, remoteness and isolation but it also symbolized above all the cultural barriers between societies.

The physical boundaries between Old World and New were turned into a metaphor for social boundedness and became the ground for a form of speculative social theory. In the background of such writing was the question of whether that insularity might ever be transcended in a universal humanity. This is the notion that Foigny puts up (and then knocks down) in the form of an imaginary society in the southern continent, building it around two related images: a personal uniformity and an absolute territorial autonomy, or nationalism.

Church ideology discouraged speculation about "other worlds" in the Middle Ages (although the Church had an exclusive one of its own). It eclipsed utopian writing and the geographical science of the Ancients, both of which, as outgrowths of commercial activity, the Church regarded as heretical as it sought to limit worldly activity in general. It asserted that lands beyond the *oikoumene,* or known world, were either unreachable, uninhabitable, or peopled by monsters. The southern continent was the limit of that unknown, repressed exterior. But in the Renaissance utopian writing was reborn as a way of exploring social theory that, as noted, gained new significance from the secrecy imposed on real explorations at that time.[1] Speculation would much later give way to science, and the global reach of empirical knowledge would sideline the utopia as a literary device. But until then it played an important role by filling gaps in Europe's knowledge of the exotic—not in the manner of a documentary report (although it usually claimed rhetorically to be one) but as an allegory; it reflected the writer's own world and its deepest concerns.

Foigny was well placed to exploit this tradition in that his own life was—like the discovery of the unknown world—a struggle against dogma. A Franciscan monk from northern France, he was unfrocked for dissolute behavior and, turning Protestant, went to Switzerland. There he found an even sterner morality and later returned to die in a Catholic monastery in Savoy. The work that preserves his name was written in the middle of this trajectory but seems, in an uncanny way, to embrace the whole. It expresses the experience many at the time (especially Huguenots)[2] shared as they migrated across the rapidly changing ideological landscape of Europe. Thus, it uses the southern-continent legend to address problems of freedom and dissent—of ideological and cultural frontiers.

1. On this aspect as it concerned the "secret discovery of Australia," see McIntyre 1977.

2. French Protestants, who at the time were persecuted in a predominantly Catholic France. Catholic activists succeeded in having Louis XIV revoke an earlier pledge of tolerance, the Edict of Nantes, in 1685.

Its apparent ambiguity about them has elicited a range of interpretations claiming it for various ideologies. A common view is that it surreptitiously promoted Enlightenment ideals of science, materialism, and natural religion or deism. But for others, it defends a traditional Christian theism or *fideism*.[3] What then were its real intentions? Was Foigny a free-thinking libertine or a right-thinking moralist? Did he favor religious toleration and social universalism or a closed society? How do such issues relate to the work's central theme of hermaphrodism, or to its geographical theme? What was Foigny's interest in the Great Southern Land?

To such questions Foigny's book yields no direct answer; like the continent itself, it remains shrouded in mystery. This ploy was common at the time—a necessity imposed by censorship. Writers exploited rhetorical devices to get a message across, often writing a bizarre novel when they might otherwise have written a tract or pamphlet. In the (exemplary) case examined here, one can refer the question of authorial intention to indications in the structure of a story in which, in the course of a utopian excursion, Foigny was able to present two separate, internally coherent worlds of thought and, thereby, cater to both the establishment and radical points of view on a range of issues.

To decide whether Foigny was a theist or deist, a futurist or primitivist, and so forth, is somewhat beside the point. As an earlier critic noted, Foigny reflects changes in French thought at the time—an invasion of the regulated, hierarchical order of the seventeenth century by the libertarian and egalitarian ideas that would dominate the eighteenth. In his thought, "Both attitudes

---

3. Fideism recognizes the validity of any organic religion; its practical counterpart is religious toleration. Deism, by contrast, seeks a "lowest common denominator" of divinity—reducing it, in other words, to a pantheistic or materialist basis. It tended to be proposed as an official religion with the rise of the modern open society as cultural relativism from the Renaissance led to a discrediting of theology, or Enlightenment.

are present. . . . He is both Christian and anti-Christian, a believer in both natural and divine law. He desires men to be equal but recognizes that they are not."[4] It is a matter, rather, of what he does with these alternatives—how the pattern of events forms a framework for interpretation and, perhaps, suggests an authorial intention. A traditional (some would say reactionary) position is represented by his hero Nicolas Sadeur; a radical, or enlightened, position, by the society he visits. Either position could be seen as a positive ideal or as a cynical parody on the author's part. To clarify the situation, I adopt a dual strategy: a search for clues in the careers of Foigny and of his book and a search for meaningful patterns within the work itself.

The Australian ethos was long interpreted as a positive ideal that Foigny was trying to promote. Critics still engaged in the emancipation from medieval patterns of life and thought saw only what they wanted to see in Foigny. His hermaphroditic theme, moreover, was construed as mere eroticism or pornography (a common motive for such imagery in earlier literature). It can now be appreciated as a metaphor for a new uniformism emerging in European life—a counterpart, on the individual level, to the rise of large centralized states, political absolutism, and religious syncretism.

Thus, his Australians are identical both physically and culturally; their religion has had all revelation refined out of it; and rationalist thought is so ingrained in them that they function like an insect society. Goods are held in common, and they are so innocent of sex that they do not even know how they procreate. Whether between each other or as a community, they know of no differences capable of arousing passion or causing conflict.

They have, in other words, achieved an ideal harmony to which ideologies down the ages have aspired—notably Christian asceticism, which many in Foigny's time (following a century of

4. Patrick (1946, 750).

bloody religious wars) had come to regard as *utopian* or even hypocritical. This contradiction, indeed, is at the heart of Sadeur's dialogues with his hermaphrodite mentor Suains. Out of it are built two opposing and irreconcilable visions of the nature of human society. Foigny's own dealings with religious authorities indicate that he knew such problems well.

The Australians' felicity also has an ethnographic basis. Confrontations between primitive and civilized society had been reported by missionaries and travelers, mainly to the Americas, and together with literary versions they would influence the *philosophes* of the Enlightenment. Foigny's naked hermaphrodites are a parody of that primitivism—of its belief in the moral superiority, egalitarianism, sincerity, and honesty of the savage. Dialogues with a "savage sage" were, as a satirical weapon against the old order in Europe, turned in the savages' favor: they were compared to the oppressed classes, whereas the hypocritical visitor represented the aristocrats and clerics who held power over them. It was natural to assume that Foigny was doing the same thing.

But missionary encounters or satirical versions of them were limited by their rhetorical stance to an either/or mode of truth. The clash of ideas was expected to lead somewhere within itself, to a kind of Hegelian absolute truth. The New World setting was, therefore, largely decorative or incidental (and could even be reversed, as in Montesquieu's *Persian Letters* of 1721, where the foreigner comes to civilization). Foigny, by contrast, lets the issues hang in ambiguity, yet his utopian décor is not at all frivolous or incidental to his polemical aims; it is crucial.

The distinction between the two worlds he presents must be made not only on the basis of the ideas themselves but also on the way they tie in with the structure of the story. They unfold within a circular progression, a cycle of departure and return. Thus, Sadeur goes to the Southern Land more or less as a victim of European history and ideology and is impressed by the alternatives he finds there but later becomes disenchanted and, finally, so much at odds with it that he has to leave. In the process not only he and his views mature but the world of ideas presented through him turns full circle.

The work relates to Enlightenment ideology, then, in a quite different way to that traditionally assumed. It outlines not an optimistic, utopian ideal but a dystopia: an anti-ideal that is visited (as one "visits" ideas) but rejected. It addresses in this way more profound issues of the status of truth in relation to time and place, of the "social construction of reality," and the way it unfolds within a specific cultural and territorial context. The variety of interpretations it has elicited owes, as mentioned, to the prestige of a bowdlerized version that suggests different conclusions than the original (all of the nine subsequent editions being that text or a translation of it). It is not certain who made these changes, but it is clear that the book was made to pander to the Enlightenment ideas that were in vogue by that time.

The original work presents those ideas, and what they sought to supplant, in an aporia—a question either unanswered or unanswerable except, as noted, by reference to factors external to the arguments themselves. The journey to the other world and back generates a narrative framework not only in the concrete sense of an imaginary voyage but also in the sense of a utopian departure from reality. During it, the hero's status relative to two opposed social worlds undergoes an evolution, and it is this framework that structures the presentation of ideas.

The work also affords a perspective on the primitivist ideals that would be prominent in Enlightenment and Romantic thought. It evokes the whole debate over whether such qualities actually existed or might be made to by the will of a people or a "legislator" (whether an elected delegate, colonial administrator, or writer of utopias). It displaces such questions onto the wider social history within which ethical forms evolve and reveals their contingent, contextual nature. This factor is what Foigny's utopia captures above all, what distinguishes it from others of its kind or period and suggests a way of approaching social and moral history in terms of processes rather than essences.

The Troubled Careers of the Author and His Work

Biographical factors play a prominent role in Foigny's book. The little known about him is mostly the result of research by Lachèvre in 1922[5] on documents related to the author's years in Switzerland (1666–1684). Born around 1630, probably in the village of Foigny in Picardy,[6] he was educated in languages, the classics, and theology. But as a monk in the strict Franciscan order of Cordeliers de l'Observance, he proved unsuited to their moral régime and at about age thirty-six (in 1666, a time of intellectual ferment generally) was expelled and fled to Calvinist Geneva. He arrived destitute, was supported for a time by the Venerable Company,[7] and renounced Catholicism before the Consistory.[8]

5. Lachèvre (1968, 1–60); on whom these biographical details and inferences are based, unless otherwise indicated.

6. Bovetti Pichetto (1976, n. 10) corrects the mistaken view (first expressed in *Journal des Sçavans,* 4 August 1692) that the village is north of Rheims in Champagne and reports details or events related to the Cistercian abbey at Foigny that resemble some found in *La Terre Australe connue.* These details do not prove, however, that the author came from there; nor was evidence found about his time in the Franciscan monastery or in a convent in Savoy. Corrected here also is the view of L. Michaud that Foigny was born at Chatillon-sur-Bar in Lorraine (like the parents of his character, Sadeur) in 1650 (*Biographie universelle,* 1816), or 1640 (*Nouvelle biographie générale,* 1857).

7. A body that Calvin set up along with the Consistory (see n. 8) to extend religious authority to the civil sphere. The Venerable Company oversaw universities, theological seminaries, and the doctrinal administration of the community. It even controlled the effective political body, a council of two hundred. It was nominally democratic and was governed by an elected moderator.

8. Composed of pastors and "elders" appointed by an inner circle of the council, the Consistory was presided over by a syndic, or chief council-

He barely scraped a living from proofreading and music teaching, and licentiousness again got him into trouble. When he broke his marriage contract with Lea Ducrest, a widow of low repute, the Consistory and Venerable Company inquired into his affairs and found him to be a libertine who debauched female servants and mixed with bad company. The City Council revoked the marriage, judged him to be in contempt of the authorities, and ordered him to leave within one week.

He went to Lausanne to begin a new teaching career. Lea joined him, and they were married, despite Geneva's opposition, because he then had residency rights there. But he did not find a position in Lausanne and survived only through the patronage of fellow expatriates: Germans, Huguenots, and others. He moved to Bern and tried to clear his reputation by writing a work of theology, *Les Attraits au service divin* (The vocation to divine service). But he could not find a publisher; such works normally were penned by pastors. He asked the city of Bern to publish it, but those engaged to read it judged it "inappropriate."[9]

Finally, in 1669 he gained a post in the College of Morges, where many Germans sent their children. Not content with this, he persisted with his *Attraits,* which were this time condemned as "infected with the spirit of Papism"[10] and again rejected. When he became first regent of the college in 1671, the Consistory tried to oust him, but he asked the authorities to examine him in theology and philosophy and emerged triumphant from this test. His persecutors then accused him of drunken behavior, such as vomiting on the communion table during a church service. His dismissal seemed imminent, so he prepared to return to Geneva and exercise his right of residence there.

This move was vigorously resisted, and when dismissed from the college, he was forbidden to leave Morges until all his debts

lor. It passed judgment on moral issues and issued recommendations to the council for action.

9. Hibner and Clerc (Bergnese theologians), cited by Lachèvre (1968, 9).

10. Consistory of Morges, cited by Lachèvre (1968, 11).

were paid. With the help of powerful friends he overcame this
harassment and even laid complaints against the Consistory and
bailiff. After an inquiry the affair was dismissed, clearing the way
for the family (now with two children and a third on the way) to
settle in Geneva. There, the Venerable Company and Consistory
tried to shut him out of a job and, although overruled by the
council, caused a split between the political and religious wings
of the government. It dragged on until reports from Morges and
Lausanne damned Foigny, and the council ceased to back him.

His career thus ruined, he carried on with private teaching
and writing. In 1673 he published in Geneva a grammar text, *La
facilité et l'élégance des langues latine et françoise* (The simplicity and
elegance of the Latin and French tongues), dedicating it to his
protector, Prince Ferdinand of Würtemberg. It was reedited in
Lyon the following year along with *L'usage du jeu royal de la langue
latine* (The royal play of the Latin tongue) and a combined edition
of the two dedicated to the Genevan councillor Marc de Roset. A
more satirical collection of magical or scientific stories, *Le Grand
Garantus,* is not extant but is thought to have appeared between
1674 and 1677.[11] A rival who was publishing a similar book
bought it up, provoking yet another quarrel, and certain passages
in it again offended the pastors. In 1674, also, Foigny added his
Attraits to an edition of psalms by the theologians Marot and Beza
and published the work without permission, again misjudging
the system. The Venerable Company impounded it and consulted the scholarchs (lay delegates to the council) about a total
ban. After another standoff with them, the council banned it,
leaving Foigny to battle for compensation.

In a state of outrage and cynicism he undertook his great
riposte, *The Southern Land, Known.* His new homeland had
revealed a doctrinal rigor and pettiness surpassing even that

---

11. Lachèvre (1968, 27). Foigny may have written a further such
work, *Le Jeu des cartes en blason.*

which he had left behind. But he would match its cunning. Claiming the author to be Sadeur himself, he told his publisher the work had come to him by way of a French bookseller named Bille (or Pille) in Clermont. Foigny asserted that it had been cleared for publication by Jean Lullin, a scholarch who had since died. The publisher, La Pierre, no doubt saw through all this but went ahead. The title page named him as "Jacques Verneuil, of Vannes," and the editor as "G. de F."

The Venerable Company pounced on the work and submitted it to theologians for a judgment on its "falsehoods, impertinences, fables, impieties and other stupidities."[12] Foigny protested that he had only translated and published the Latin manuscript for the French bookseller, who now had all the copies. The place of publication had been falsified on the recommendation of Lullin, in whose view Sadeur wrote "more like a Papist than a Huguenot"[13] (an ironical twist—if true, this would have defeated the purpose of publishing the book outside France). As for the indecency of the naked hermaphrodites, Foigny insisted that it was plain ethnographic truth.

But the pastors were not to be taken in. La Pierre was asked to produce the manuscript and proof of Lullin's permission and Foigny to identify the bookseller and declare whether or not he himself shared the Australians' ideas. La Pierre stated that he had sent all the copies to Foigny and had only seen Lullin's permission, and Foigny named Bille, or Pille (again, perhaps an ironical reference to the "bilious" nature of the work), and said that he regarded the Australians' fables "in the same light as one would the revelations of the Koran."[14] He, too, said he no longer had the letter of permission, and the matter was referred to the council for legal action. The Company had Bille, or Pille, investigated and

---

12. Pastor Amy Mestrezat, cited by Lachèvre (1968, 35).
13. Lachèvre (1968, 39).
14. Ibid.

tried to close La Pierre's press. Foigny may have bought time by getting councillors to read the work, and the first syndic may have had his own reasons for opposing the Company. But when in March 1677 it was learned that the Bille, or Pille, story was false, the pair were arrested on charges of fraud and impiety.

Foigny repeated his story and invoked the opinion of another dead witness that the work was "by some melancholic."[15] Although admitting to some frivolity in his dealings with the Company, he pleaded his allegiance to the Reformed faith and the poverty of his family and was released for a few days. He then prepared an action for wrongful arrest, and the trial was adjourned. The book was not banned, and his powerful friends persuaded the Company to drop its case. He also rode out allegations of involvement in a fraud case in Bordeaux, and the council allowed him to remain in Geneva for as long as it pleased the syndics. He seems to have been, in all of this, a pawn in a wider struggle between religious and secular forces in the Genevan government.

In 1684, now a widower, he was accused of getting his servant Jeanne Berlie pregnant. They denied the charge before the Consistory but were ordered to separate. The child was born a Catholic, Jeanne having converted, and Foigny, too, declared that his persecutors had driven him to reconvert along with all his children. The latter were then seized, and their godparents enlisted to keep them in the Reformed faith. But when no one would take charge of them, the case was referred to the French authorities. Foigny was then allowed to reclaim his children, sell his house, and leave. But he found only three of the children; his daughter Catherine he never saw again (the Genevan archives mention her in 1693 and his second son, Anthoine, in 1688).

He retired to a Catholic monastery in Savoy and died there in 1692. In that year appeared an anonymous, abridged version of

15. Quoting Professor Louis Tronchin (Lachèvre 1968, 46).

his book, *Les Avantures de Jacques Sadeur dans la découverte et le voiage de la Terre Australe.* It is not known whether he died before or after it was printed or whether the revision was by himself, by the presumed editor (Abbé François Raguenet), or by someone else. Lachèvre attributes it to a Foigny eager for notoriety and seeking to publish the work at whatever cost to its original integrity.[16] If, as it seems, Foigny believed in 1676 that the original work would vindicate him, the problem of deciding how—what his ideas actually were—invites a comparison with the changes made in 1692 and the question of who made them.[17]

These changes, apart from rationalizing somewhat its style and spelling, radically altered the work ideologically. As noted, the ambivalence of the deistic and Christian arguments was lost; the new version truncated the latter to the point where the former overwhelmed it. Not only was this more in step with Englightenment trends but it did much to ground the traditional view that Foigny's message was a pro-Enlightenment one: a view that reflects both a normative tendency to rewrite the past in terms of the present and the interpretation suggested by the 1692 version, which most critics used until the twentieth century.[18]

Raguenet seems[19] to have been a deist, a *mondain,* or society cleric, who welcomed Enlightenment trends. The book may have

16. Lachèvre (1968, 60). Patrick also thinks the 1692 changes were made by Foigny (Negley and Patrick 1952, 401), as does Garagnon (1984, 51–53). A Further such indication is discussed on p. 144 under "The 1692 Version" of the bibliography.

17. The substantial changes are noted in editions of the 1676 text by Lachèvre (1968) and Ronzeaud (1990), but there has not been a combined or recent edition of the 1692 text that would show the many detailed changes.

18. As pointed out by Adam (1962, 323–24) and Ronzeaud (1982a, 20, 70). Benrekassa (1980, 265), however, discounts the difference between the two texts. Kirsop (1980) demonstrates a greater distribution of the 1676 version than had been thought.

19. Storer (1945a, 283–96; Storer 1945b).

provided him with a means of propagating such radical ideas at no risk to himself (just as Foigny had tried to distance himself from it). It seems unlikely that Foigny himself would have made such drastic changes to his work; had he merely wanted notoriety, for example, he could have published the original in Holland in his own name, as was common with radical works. To rename the hero "Jacques Sadeur" (originally the hero's father) also seems a gratuitous distortion, and the revision generally is a crude reduction of an already compact and highly structured text.

Both textual and contextual indications thus suggest that Raguenet adapted the work to his own polemical ends around the time Foigny died. An alternative explanation, that Foigny himself had come to espouse Australian ideas, is inconsistent with the nature of the changes made and with the original sophistication of his hermaphrodite theme, his narrative and dialogical progression, and other elements. Their reduction to a relatively simplistic and popular argument suggests either the intervention of a lesser talent or a degeneration of Foigny's intellect. It is also, notes Ronzeaud,[20] inconsistent with his residence in a monastery, nor is he likely to have done it for stylistic or typographical reasons, having shown little concern with such details elsewhere. No evidence exists that he left a revised manuscript at his death.

Storer traces the link with Raguenet through bibliographies such as Barbier's *Dictionnaire des ouvrages anonymes* (1822–1827) or Quérard's *Supercheries littéraires dévoilées* (Literary hoaxes unveiled) to the eighteenth-century bibliographers Moreri and Ladvocat.[21] She also notes that the Bibliothèque Nationale copy of the 1676

20. Ronzeaud (1982a, 325–26).

21. Quérard noted that Ladvocat (*Dictionnaire historique et bibliographique,* "Raguenet" article) had attributed the original to Gabriel de Frogny *{sic},* correcting assumptions that Raguenet was the original author (Ronzeaud 1990, xxviii). Quérard himself apparently believed that Sadeur was the author (such confusion of an author with a fictional narrator commonly dogged the reception of anonymous imaginary voyages).

text came from Falconet, formerly a physician to the Bouillon family, where Raguenet served as a tutor. So Raguenet may have come by the text there (although it was probably widely available [see n. 18]). Again, Raguenet's other works indicate that his early interest in theology progressed toward others (such as exotism and militarism) that are found in Foigny's story and preserved in the new edition, whereas its theological aspect is mutilated.

Whether or not Raguenet edited the 1692 text, the criticism based on it is now a subject of critical debate. Thus, Pierre Bayle, a Huguenot exile in Rotterdam, was the first to study the work seriously. He associated it with the hermaphrodism in Gen. 2 (that of Adam before the Fall), Plato's *Symposium,* Ovid's *Metamorphoses,* Thomas Browne's *Religio Medici* (1635), or the French mystic Antoinette Bourignon, a contemporary of Foigny who wrote that "sin has disfigured in man the work of God. . . . Instead of men being what they should be, they have become monsters in nature, divided into two imperfect sexes, unable to reproduce themselves alone—as do trees and plants, which in this respect are more perfect than men or women."[22] But Bayle was apparently unaware that Bourignon wrote three years after Foigny, and as a strong advocate of Enlightenment ideas, he saw only the latter in the Sadeur story—both conclusions probably resulting from his use of the 1692 version.

In the early eighteenth century the story of "James Sadeur" aroused some curiosity along with similar works by Henry Neville (*The Isle of Pines,* 1668), Denis Vairasse (see n. 28), Simon Tyssot de Patot (*Le voyage et avantures de Jaques Massé,* ca. 1710), or Hendrik Smeeks (*Beschryvinge van het magtig koningryk Krinke Kesmes,* 1708). These authors were Huguenots or had otherwise

22. Bayle (1697, 987 ff., "Sadeur" article) citing (989–91) Bourignon's *Le Nouveau ciel et la nouvelle terre* (Amsterdam, 1679). On Foigny's sources for the hermaphrodite theme see Ronzeaud (1982a, 19–84), and on his use of it Guicciardi (1980, 57) and Leibacher-Ouvrard (1984, 1989). Benrekassa (1980, 264) notes that Bayle seems to have used only the 1692 edition.

experienced persecution, and all related a pseudo-real visit to the Great Southern Land—one made all the more piquant by the fact that spectacular real encounters with Australia had occurred during the seventeenth century but were known to the public only as hearsay owing to policies of official secrecy. In the absence of published accounts, it was impossible to disprove what a novelist might claim to be a true story, and many did believe them—especially that of Vairasse. The same would later be true of *Robinson Crusoe* and other Robinsonades.

Satirical writers played this problematization of the truth to the limit, a phenomenon that would have great consequences for literature and thought during the eighteenth century. The narrative form and rhetorical stance they pioneered would spawn numerous utopias and imaginary voyages—most of inferior quality but some (such as those of Defoe and Swift) that would exert an immense influence. The doubt and suspicion their works aroused, by relativizing the truth, can be seen too in the case of Foigny; a 1705 edition was allowed, for example, only "on condition that it be regarded purely as a novel."[23]

Earlier critics did not make this connection with historical events (literary realism has only recently been theorized in this way, and the role in it of the "austral" novels has not been examined in depth). Apart from the bibliographers mentioned, few knew of the work by the late eighteenth century, and the last edition in 1788 was in an anthology of early "curiosities." In the nineteenth century, moreover, such works came to be seen as forerunners of the utopian socialism of Fourier, Cabet, and others (anachronistic readings, especially of Foigny),[24] or as libertarian

23. "A considérer cet ouvrage comme un pur Roman, l'impression peut en être permise." Pouchart (*Approbation,* 4 Dec. 1704). Cited by Lachèvre (1968, 166). On the subject of the austral novels and their role in the rise of eighteenth-century realism, see Fausett 1993.

24. Cf. Lichtenberger (1885, 39–40), Girsberger (1924, 111–12), Van Wijngaarden (1932, 15, 76–79), and (stressing the aspect of monastic communism) Africa (1979, 54–56, 219–20).

tracts.[25] Early in this century, Lanson (1908) saw the work as an "early manifestation of the philosophical spirit," an approach developed by his pupil, Atkinson, and by Chinard and Lachèvre. These critics also focused on the erotic aspect, tending to write off Foigny as a vulgar rake. Atkinson interpreted his hermaphrodism as feminism and the religious aspect as an argument for deism and considered the work "the most poorly composed story of the type published before 1720."[26] However, these critics generally used the 1676 text.

Such views prevailed until the 1970s, when revised theories of utopianism, the realist novel, and the role of the narrator and narrative structure in such works began to cast that of Foigny in a new light; more was to be found here than a blithe dream of Enlightenment. Cioranescu (1972, 158-60) pointed to an element of pessimism in it, building on a view expressed by Chinard in 1913 (205). Benrekassa (1974) analyzed its narrative and (1978) its anthropological interest, and others discussed its status as a novel, a utopia, or an imaginary voyage.[27] In general, these readings revealed a greater coherence of the work, notably in its use of the metaphor of hermaphrodism, than had previously been suspected. As a result of the biographical information provided by Lachèvre and others, it also became evident how closely this textual coherence was bound up with the author's own life experience.

25. Lanson (1907–8, 11–15; 1908, 146–47). This aspect was also emphasized in 1897 by Nettlau (1968), by another anarchist critic, Berneri (1950, 197), and by Rihs (1970, 337).

26. Atkinson 1922 (15–19, 24n; cf. also Atkinson 1920, 56, 85, 106). Gove (1941, 98–108) discusses the problem of categorizing imaginary voyages and utopias and shows Atkinson's influence.

27. Coulet 1967; Trousson 1974, 1975, 1977, 1978; Demoris 1975 (165–69, 174–76); Chupeau 1977. Benrekassa's contributions are reproduced in his 1980 monograph, cited here. Ronzeaud (1982a) offered an interpretation in terms of positive polemics, which has been revised (1990).

Atkinson had earlier divined such significance and called this the "first complete novel of *Extraordinary Voyage* known" and its use of a hermaphroditic society to solve social and moral problems "original, but perhaps not as fantastic as would appear today" (1920, 163). Although Foigny was by no means original in either respect, Atkinson did much to foster the rethinking of Foigny and others of his kind. Indeed, Foigny's contemporary, Vairasse, had earlier been recognized as the bearer of a new rhetorical mode in a path-breaking essay by Tieje (1913) and would remain the primary or better-known example of it.[28] More recently, major studies of literary realism in general have done much to elucidate its aesthetic or intellectual ramifications.[29]

Recent Foigny criticism has tended to draw out, in effect, the implications of that cautious *imprimatur* of 1705. What follows builds on this foundation, focusing on his use of geographical realism. Such an approach can facilitate the interpretation of other themes and of the work as a coherent whole and bears as well on the wider debate over the nature of utopian writing. The incomprehension that earlier greeted this and other works of its kind owed mainly to an attempt to force them into the mold of the "English utopia"—that product of seventeenth-century England and its political upheavals, that, building on an aspect of the tradition derived from Plato and others, offered an imaginary society as a positive model for emulation—a program for political reconstruction. But a whole current of early utopian writing was doing nothing of the sort.

---

28. Cf. Von der Mühll (1938), Demoris (1974, 165, 378), or Racault (1991, pt. 2, chap. 2), who considers the *History of the Sevarites* the "paradigm text" for the whole production of voyage utopias during the century of Enlightenment. See also n. 38.

29. See Fausett 1993, chap. 10.

The Utopian Paradigm: A Problem of Boundaries

Boundaries in Space

Foigny's utopia reflects a grasp of narrative procedures and a knowledge of geopolitical trends, and it was motivated by biographical factors. How do these elements relate to themes and devices within the work? As noted, a rhetorical stance is elaborated by way of a narrative development based, in turn, on a real structure of events and experiences. If these layers of construction are linked in some significant way, how is it manifested? Was the author consciously aware of it?

In fact, he had inherited such a paradigm—apart from its evident parallels with biblical allegory—from the history of European contact with the New World. Among his possible sources one finds a long tradition of satirical voyages to other worlds, from Hellenistic models (and, of course, Plato's utopia, Atlantis) and that of Lucian in late Antiquity[30] to More and Rabelais in the Renaissance or writers in Foigny's own century: Campanella, Godwin, Cyrano de Bergerac, and others.

Some critics also recognize medieval sources: cosmographies such as the *Imago Mundi* (Image of the world), Arthurian romances, or (for Foigny's giant birds) the Nordic Kraken or the "rukh" reported by Marco Polo.[31] By contrast with Vairasse's

---

30. Foigny's debt to ancient (mainly Hellenistic) narrative models is discussed in Fausett 1990 and 1993. On the satirical charge inherent in travel literature, see Adams (1962, 1982); and on utopia's more indirectly satirical bearing (as allegory), see Elliott (1970, 3–23). As Elliott points out, satire and utopia are two facets of the same basic rhetorical device, the questioning of an existing norm by suggesting an alternative one.

31. Chinard (1970, 197n.); Kuon (1987, 263; 1986, 317–21). Bovetti Pichetto (1976, 377n.) identifies as a major source (along with biblical ones) the popular story of St. Brendan's voyage to America. Ronzeaud (1982a, chap. 2) discusses Foigny's likely geographical sources.

contemporary *History of the Sevarites,* for example, Foigny's utopia is "more involved with the Middle Ages than the century of Enlightenment: both aesthetically, in that it doubles the literal meaning of the text with an allegorical meaning; and ideologically, in that it categorically denies . . . any possibility of human and social perfection in the fallen world that is ours (and) is a purely formal authentification."[32] Later, missionaries or travelers reported and discussed savage nudity (see chap. 5, n. 15; chap. 6, n. 3), and this also contributed to an allegorical bearing, both in primitivist thought and in literary parodies of it. Even the phenomenon of hermaphrodism itself was among the "monstrosities" reported by travelers to the New World.[33]

Indeed, Foigny's work is a parody of serious erudition in the Menippean tradition (named after a freed slave in Antiquity, who became a Cynical philosopher and novelist). Two other works in that style had appeared in 1605 and are likely sources for his hermaphrodite theme: Joseph Hall's *Mundus alter et idem* (A world other and the same) and *L'Isle des Hermaphrodites* by Thomas Arthus. Hall describes a southern-land dystopia with an offshore Hermaphrodite Island, whereas Arthus more explicitly develops sexual inversion as a metaphor for moral degeneration, again within the framework of an imaginary voyage. Although the basic tradition was here again an ancient one, these baroque works drew an explicit relation between hermaphrodism and travel to unknown places, particularly to the antipodes. The latter epitomized the foreign—a geospatial "other" that implied absolute cultural difference and the psychological or moral alienation experienced (as Europeans were finding out) by the visitor to such places.

Foigny's acknowledged source is the famous Pedro Fernandez de Quirós (1560–1614), a Portuguese pilot in the Spanish navy who claimed to have found the southern continent while in

32. Kuon (1987, 268–69).
33. Atkinson (1920, 58).

Melanesia in 1605–1606 (not 1610, as Foigny states). He found, in fact, Espiritu Santo Island in Vanuatu (formerly the New Hebrides). He tried to interest the crown in colonizing this land by portraying it as an earthly paradise and naming it "Austrialia del Espiritu Santo" (the austral-Austria-land of the Holy Spirit), a pun intended to flatter the Austrian-based Habsburg monarchy. It failed to impress the authorities but was destined for a great literary career and even appeared on early maps of the Queensland coast. It was also the origin of the name Australia, which appears for the first time in print in *La Terre Australe connue.* The eighth of Quirós' fourteen *requestes* appeared in Latin in De Bry's voyage-collection of 1613 and then, because of its popularity, in French in the journal *Mercure de France* (1617) and later in voyage collections such as Thévenot's,[34] which fostered French ambitions in the New World.

As various critics have noted, it was only necessary for Foigny and others to press home this ready-made realism. Some have identified his source for the Congo episode as the visit of Magellan's companions Pigafetta and Lopez, as found in De Bry.[35] Like Quirós, however, they had crossed the Pacific from America, whereas Sadeur's voyage seems to be based on accounts of voyages to the East Indies via Africa and the Indian Ocean. Dutch rutters of this route, such as Linschoten's *Itinerario* of 1595, contain descriptions of the storm-swept latitudes, idyllic islands, and exotic flora and fauna Foigny describes.

34. De Bry 1598–1628; Thévenot 1663. See Atkinson (1920, 76–80).

35. Trousson (1974, 375–76). Ronzeaud (1982a, 126–34) questions this, and suggests as alternatives Thévenot, the cosmographer André Thevet, or a range of sources including Jean de Léry and others who reported French—largely Huguenot—activity in the Americas (on which, see Lestringant 1990). The travels of Jean Mocquet (Paris, 1616) may have been a source for the Madagascar episode or other "austral" elements in the work. On early Indian Ocean writings Foigny may have known, see Linon 1988, 1990.

They were based in turn, initially, on lore deriving from the earlier Portugese presence in the region. The Dutch had access to this through their links with the Spanish Habsburg empire and used it in taking over the East Indies trade early in the seventeenth century. The intensity of Dutch activity then resulted in further accounts, such as the popular memoirs of Willem Bontekoe, a sea captain with the Dutch East India Company who was there in the years 1618–1625.[36] Even in Foigny's lifetime, Dutch activities provided a scenario suited to his literary purposes. Abel Tasman's great discoveries in 1642–1644 had failed to "make known" the eastern parts of Australia and New Zealand; questions remained, such as whether the lands were part of the legendary great continent. As an ethnographic unknown, too, the latter remained essentially unchanged.

Accounts of travel in these parts often bordered so closely on the fantastic as to contain the seeds of a utopian paradigm. A 1701 Dutch work, for example, contained both a true account of a visit to Australia (a ship's journal) and translations of the utopias of Foigny and Vairasse, which many believed were also true descriptions of societies encountered there.[37] The East Indies route was, furthermore, a circular trajectory of departure from a known world, entry into an unknown one, and a "miraculous" return after facing its many hazards. By contrast with travel to the Americas, it was also a narrowly circumscribed path; accounts of it (whether real or imaginary) included a regular series of landfalls (the Canary or Cape Verde Islands, St. Helena, the Cape of Good Hope, Madagascar, and so on), often made in both directions on the same voyage. This sea route was, in other words, the primary model for the formal narrative symmetry that became a "utopian paradigm."[38]

36. Translated and introduced in Bontekoe 1929.

37. See "Translations" under "The Text and Related Editions" of the bibliography.

38. Cf. n. 28: Vairasse's work, similar in this respect, was published in London in 1675, then in an augmented edition (which may have drawn

Boundaries of Culture

That symmetry of both theme and form had, as noted, appeared with Hellenistic predecessors, whose imaginary voyages in the Indian Ocean also resemble in other ways that of Foigny. It had been refined by More and others into a procedure of narrative doubling: the insertion of an inner— usually utopian—story into an outer, authenticating (because purportedly authentic) one. This device distanced an author from direct responsibility for his work, and, apart from being convenient in times of strict censorship (such as those Foigny lived in), helped to make meaningful links between a works's various levels of reference. It doubled the outer, geospatial excursion with an analogous one at the psychological level— one with a real basis, too, in the experience of traveling merchants, sailors, missionaries, or (like Foigny) exiles and refugees within Europe itself.

Sadeur's austral adventure is a classic example of this effect, transposing a narrative at the scenic level onto the plane of intellectual ideas. His experience of displacement (or, rather, "dys-placement") is projected onto a global screen to become a statement about the human condition—life is an excursion into a world of ideas, which often prove uncongenial. He is the archetypal European of an age of absolutism and (as a related effect) of an age of exploration—a modern Odysseus, the prophet of a new world of mobility.

Grandoise as such pretentions may seem, they are evident in the work. Sadeur's adventures proceed from his catastrophic early life through a series of (symbolic) shipwrecks, in the

---

further inspiration from Foigny) in Paris in 1677–1679. The wider questions raised by their simultaneous use of an "austral" hyper-realism are discussed in Fausett 1993. The hallmark of their style, for example—the famous authentifying preface—clearly had a maritime source. It is examined in the case of Vairasse by Bourez (1984).

course of which he becomes adept at surviving such disasters. Carried away by a violent storm and wrecked in the southern ocean, he saves himself on a plank in a parody of Christ's crucifixion.[39] He gains access to the southern continent by his victory over the giant birds that are the Australians' dreaded enemies, and as a further result, he arrives among them naked—symbolically reborn in the manner traditional among classical utopias. It is also providential that he is a hermaphrodite like them because this land is as exclusive as the Heaven it parodies; any "half-men," or monosexuals, who arrive there are usually killed immediately.

But his hermaphrodism is really a metaphor for his ability to embrace ambiguity and duality in a conceptual or cultural sense. It is this quality that enables him to be accepted, and the metaphor expressing it again facilitates the paradigm shift mentioned; it translates relationships in the natural and cultural worlds onto the psychological level. It ties in with other themes and details; for example, his later reversion to "normal" masculinity (when confronted with a female prisoner of war after thirty-five years of abstinence) precipitates his fall from grace and return to the real world. A circularity of excursion into fantasy and return to reality thus extends beyond the merely scenic to illustrate the way cultural and mental worlds are structured. A similar pattern is found, interestingly, in Arthus's earlier hermaphrodite utopia.[40]

---

39. Racault (1991, V:1) notes similarities between this series of symbolic disasters, which relate to oedipal distortions of Sadeur's personality, his guilt complex and exile from society as a "monster," and those found in *Robinson Crusoe*. Indeed, the new view of Foigny's Australian society as an inhuman (rather than "ideal") society shows how close it was to the *absence* of society found in *Robinson Crusoe*. Again, new evidence of the notoriety of Foigny and others in Defoe's day reinforces internal evidence suggesting that the latter owed much to that prior tradition.

40. See Fausett 1993, chap. 3.

This play of the real and imaginary is anchored in the earth itself by the theme of a voyage to the austral regions and back. The difference between these two spaces, or worlds, is again mediated by an in-between form, or "halfway house,"[41] analogous to hermaphrodism. One of these is visited on the way to the Southern Land and another on the way back (as on the real East Indies route). They underline the transition from one cultural world to another. In the first of these interludes, Sadeur explores the heart of Africa and reports in realist tones what he finds: a nature run wild and a human apathy or degeneracy that he blames on tropical abundance. It forms a relay or springboard relative to the surreal, "antipodean" (inverted) world of the Southern Land, where an artificial perfection of the environment is accompanied by a cultural activism carried to extremes—a human perfection.

Later he regains civilization via Madagascar, which is again situated midway between nature and culture, reason and madness, savagery and civilization. A hint of ethnographic realism can be detected when he meets a captured chief from an island somewhere in the region. When the chief dies of grief at being stuck in this "no-man's-land"—unable either to return home or to accompany Sadeur to Europe—his compatriots, too, commit suicide, and their corpses, thrown into the sea, all unite and miraculously drift back to their island. This little parody—whether of the social cohesion primitivists attributed to such peoples or of the concept of an afterlife—forms a realist echo of the world Sadeur has left (and also recalls his arrival there, borne on a magic current).

41. Demoris (1975, 168). Rosenberg, too, notes that such digressions "far from being irrelevant, formed an integral part of the attempt to convey either an impression of authenticity or to illustrate some aspect of the ideal society. That is to say that these digressions cannot be removed without doing damage to the author's main purpose of describing a utopia" (1972, 125; cf. also Rosenberg 1971).

It also presages his own death, related at the outset in a "Notice to the Reader." Arriving at Livorno in Italy, he slips off the gangplank and soon after dies, bequeathing his manuscript to the "editor." This closes the circle not only of Sadeur's life but of the many themes opened during his adventures. The cycle of life and death, indeed, proves to be a master theme subsuming and completing all the other dichotomies of place, gender, or culture here opened to question as a field of ideas analogous to the surface of the globe. Death, the universal closure, is what Sadeur finds at the heart of the austral world.

His dialogues with the venerable Suains compare European and Australian society. Central to them is the contradiction between the principles of unity that Europeans profess and the reality of sectarian or nationalist violence that Sadeur admits is normal. The Australians have transcended such inconsistencies; they form a monoculture, untroubled by any kind of difference. As a utopia in the strict (spatial) sense, the continent has no borders; they cannot even conceptualize a social boundary, let alone associate it with a physical one. Even the land itself has been "homogenized," leveled into an escarpment evenly descending from pole to coast, as a result of which (and owing to a baroque cosmology) the climate, too, is uniform. Their life is rigorously structured both in time and space. Geometrical buildings embody a complex hierarchy of symbolic materials from floor to roof and from garden to temple, a translucent rock crystal that reflects their social-insect rationality and their deistic metaphysics.[42] Their nudity, a parody of the "moral transparency" (sincerity,

42. Apart from biblical sources (cf. Rev. 21) and real models, such as the stepped pyramids of the Incas or in Southeast Asia, this may echo ancient Roman town planning based on religious principles. Cf. too the Australians' "contemplation" of divinity: a word derived from the Latin *templum,* originally meaning a space marked out by the augur for the divinatory observation of birds and, hence, a sanctuary, temple, or shrine. (Rykwert 1988, 98–99)

honesty, and equality) that primitivists associated with savage society, adds to this effect. In these ways Foigny bridges the gap between the abstract and concrete, or cultural and natural, aspects of his utopia.

Boundaries of Human Life

But these long-lived and serene beings are afflicted with existential anguish and practice "philosophical suicide." As the dialogues proceed, it becomes clear that Sadeur's enthusiasm for their world is fading. He finds flaws in its basic philosophical principles, and he and Suains eventually agree to differ. This part of the work (chap. 6) was, significantly, the one most mutilated in the 1692 edition; its original sense was almost obliterated. Finally, a long chapter on the Australians' periodic wars makes it clear that they do have real borders and enemies. Among their halfling enemies are "sea monsters" (Europeans), who arrive in ships from places unknown to them. Here fiction begins to engage again with historical reality, portending Sadeur's return to Europe and the closure of the utopian circle.

The reality he rejoins is ultimately that of the material dimension itself—the real world or, on the psychological level, the realities of bodily existence. The Southern Land and its ethos are essentially a metaphysical problem "fleshed out" in all its cultural or anthropological implications. In the same way that the Australians' ideas about their nation and its boundaries are illusory, they avoid facing that ultimate boundary, death. Carried away by their rationalist powers, they live in a cocoon of abstractions, a kind of collective autism. They regard all physical functions as shameful and irrational; even their manner of procreating remains a mystery because they never discuss it. Sadeur opposes to this world of illusion the reality he knows— that of a negotiated compromise with the mortality of the flesh and with its desires (as a flesh divided by the duality of sex).

The Australians' Fundian enemies are normal in this respect and inspire in them a horror that leads them to commit the most irrational cruelties. But their deadliest enemies are the Urgs, which ravage them most violently during their rut; halberds and shields are little defense against them. It is by taming one of these that Sadeur eventually escapes from the continent—fittingly, for the Urgs are the supreme representatives of the physical dimension. As mentioned, the Australians' fears that Sadeur is really a half-man are confirmed during a war with the Fundians when he commits the "original sin" with a captive girl (and fails to collect a string of Fundian ears). Sentenced to death by suicide, he delays it long enough to tame an Urg and fly out on it—a graphic illustration of what the development of the dialogues pointed to in philosophical terms, his ability to negotiate with the "facts of life."

The crux of the encounter occurs in chapter 5. Discussing the binarity of sex and whether it poses (or symbolizes) an obstacle to dialectical reason, the pair reach an impasse over the definition of humanity itself. The nature-culture problem is here bound up with gender (as, for example, in modern debates over the use of *man* as a synonym for humanity, and so on). If, Suains points out, that traditional view of humanity is based on the exploitation of one sex by the other (and, by implication, would remain exploitative even if inverted), what alternative is there but a society of hermaphrodites? A similar impasse is encountered when Sadeur attempts to explain concepts such as a father, mother, or family; Suains conceptualizes human existence in purely physical terms and as something beyond any question of origins (other than in a materialist "first principle," the supreme being posited by deism).

Sadeur rejects this logic, not out of sexism or religious dogmatism but because he feels his own logic to be superior (although he expresses it rather poorly). He rejects the radical individualism of the hermaphrodites, whose denial of reciprocity at the level of sex and reproduction doubles their utopian irreality at the level of the community—their illusion of living without boundaries. Initially, it seemed that the problems of sex relations and family life had been overcome by having no social structures come between the individual and the state. This ideal is later deconstructed along with the utopia as a whole as it is inserted back into worldly reality.

Sadeur's scepticism is, thus, vindicated. In terms of the cyclical paradigm (real-irreal-real), he is the one who sees through to its end and accepts things that are inevitable, whereas his utopian hosts are caught halfway. This quality relates to his ambiguous nature, alluded to earlier—his ability to straddle two worlds of ideas or existence and encompass them dialectically. Hence, too, the revelation that his hermaphrodism is merely metaphorical by contrast with the literal, physical hermaphrodism of the Australians (or the homosexuality that was traditionally associated with metaphors of hermaphrodism). It signifies an understanding that extends from the plurality of worlds[43] down to dualities of nature and culture and even of life and death.

One recalls, in this connection, his catastrophic childhood: torn from his family, that mediating barrier against the world, he experiences the latter with a directness that leaves him with an uncommon sense of the physical side of life and of its mortality. His psyche, rather than progressing through a gradual repression of that original experience, is thrust immediately into the realm of culture and remains thereafter split between culture and its prior allegiance to nature. Thus, he encounters Braganza ambushers as "inhuman beasts, worse than flesh-crazed wolves" and sees the Congo as a natural paradise where human virtues of vigor and industry are extinguished. He lives in perilous contact

---

43. A subject of interest to philosophers of the day, both as a problem of astronomy and of sociology; cf., for example, Fontenelle's *Entretien sur la pluralité des mondes* (1686).

with the animal and even mineral worlds, as expressed by his "amphibian" qualities: his intimate relationship with the sea, his obsession with flying fish and other amphibious creatures, riverine societies, the impact of rain or wave action on landforms, and so forth.

Boundaries of Representation

As Sadeur puts it, he was "conceived in America and born upon the ocean, a too telling presage of what I would one day become." This revealing comment underlines the implication noted: that he was intended to be an archetypal figure bearing all the significance of the Old World's experience of the New. At the global level as at the personal, he remains acutely aware of the natural basis for human culture, an understanding that stands him in good stead as he progresses from his early experience of political conflict to that of the utopia. The Southern Land symbolizes the New World in general in that Europe's relationship with the latter was ushering in a new mode of human existence based on commerce rather than traditional communitarian concerns. That relationship is a central theme in the work, tying all its others into a general theory of boundaries and forming a pivot that articulates its two levels of realism, biographical and geopolitical.

Sadeur's voyage to the Southern Land thus allegorizes his age's experience of the discovery of Australasia, the last great geographical unknown. This discovery was significant for economic or geopolitical reasons (the hope—or fear—of finding another America) but also had wider symbolic significance: here the Old World would assimilate its last major "other" and evolve into a modern geopolitical entity, the West, defined in terms of relative economic development rather than the differences between whole societies owing to their isolation. The barriers penetrated in this process were the sea and the limited state of maritime technology. The sea had always played a special role in writings about the relations between societies because it represented a medium of communication no less crucial in this literary context than in the "real" world of commerce and trade.

Sadeur's mastery of it is doubled, moreover, by his proficiency in that other medium of communication, language. As mentioned, it is his uniquely bifid understanding—his figural hermaphrodism—that enables him to enter another world, learn its secrets, and return to tell the tale. The sea and language share, as media, a dual function of facilitation and exclusion—an ambivalence that is inherent in any kind of communication. The play on boundaries that pervades this utopia is uppermost too in the artificial language Foigny invented for it. As a grammarian and linguist, he was clearly familiar with the philosophical problems of individuals and universals, the material and social aspects of the signifying process, nature and convention. Is meaning immanent in the (material) sign itself or dependent primarily on a relationship between language users? Does the "inscriptional trace" come before spoken language or vice versa? Sadeur seems, for example, to imply the latter when he mentions that he has decided to "reduce" his story to writing.

Again, his problematical status among the Australians is reflected in linguistic distortions, which presage the "disorders" that eventually oblige him to leave. Their language, of course, is totally rational and uniform—a cratylist or universal scheme, like others invented at the time. It vowels and consonants each name a specific object or quality and are arranged into signifying combinations that cover every concept ever encountered by an Australian. Confusion is eliminated along with the arbitrary nature of real languages. In fact, their communication is so standardized that it often proceeds by gesture, using signs that emanate directly from the body.

The material aspect of this artificial language—its sounds or written marks—is assimilated to the same spatial paradigm as applies in the case of lands, people, or ideas. Bits of meaning are harnessed together to form, hieroglyphically, whole meanings. These, being of identical value everywhere, are structurally analogous to the society itself as a "syntax" or configuration of language users. Here, more than in other cratylist schemes, significance is vested in the form of the sign itself, a system not unlike musical notation (Foigny taught music, and the job he was refused in Geneva was as a church singer. Rousseau's later fascination with written music would similarly complement his interests in language and society).

This effect is reinforced by the language's onomatopoeic basis: a sweet apple is *ipm,* an unpleasant fruit, *ird.* There is no room here for cultural difference: the biblical connotations of *apple,* for example, cannot be represented by such a system (the Australian concept of fruit, in any case, appears to derive from the vegetal theme found in early materialist philosophies). Critics have noted how this ideal language differs from that of Vairasse, which reflects the empiricist, a posteriori bias of his utopia—its derivation from real cultural elements—whereas that of Foigny is an a priori proposition abstracted from reality.[44]

Here again one encounters boundaries as a process of inclusion and exclusion. Metaphor, the "carrying beyond" of meaning, is anathema to the Australians because it opens language to outside correspondences. Their concern with literality is, thus, related to their myth of autonomy, their closed society, their inability to accept any existential order based on exchange and reciprocity, even that of a father and mother. And just as parenting is for them a purely physical affair, so their language too has a purely material basis.

44. Pellandra (1986, 55–71). Cf. this volume chap. 9, n. 1 and introduction, n. 46. Leibacher-Ouvrard (1989, 31) notes that the Moravian theorist Comenius had outlined in *Via Lucis* (1672) the options available to language-builders: either a recasting of existing languages (like that of Vairasse) or a radical break into artificiality (as by Foigny).

What Foigny offers here is a semiotic theory. One might, for example, see affinities between this Australian concept of the sign and modern attempts to invert the traditional priority of spoken over written language or ethical over material aspects of the semiotic process.[45] Here again, it is essential to bear in mind that it forms part not of a eutopia but of a dystopia; it is bracketed and placed under the sign of the negative, so to speak, by a controlling framework of excursion and return—a utopian paradigm.

Boundaries of Reason

A similar situation prevails in the areas of metaphysics and religion. Like language, religious ideology acts (in the real world) as a marker of cultural differences. Both reflect, and ultimately derive from, differences of territory, and at the level of the community as a whole they reflect a more general boundary, that with the material world—the nature-culture dichotomy. Thus, when Sadeur explains that religion takes two forms in Europe— a deistic one based on ancient materialisms and a theistic or "revealed" one—it is deism that Suains approves as the only system able to transcend the divisive effects of local difference.

But as Sadeur tries to elaborate on revealed religion, the common ground begins to give way and with it his admiration for the apparent rationality and elegance of the Australian system. Their logic is impeccable, but irrelevant; it is suited only

45. As by Derrida (1976), who agues that the inscriptional trace logically precedes the phonic sign. Indeed, the deconstructionist gesture of putting the ostensible "under erasure" is analogous to the utopian passage to another world. And just as the latter must be completed by a return to reality, so the notion of a priority of writing over speech rests on a logical fallacy: a confusion of the orders of experience and its communication, of the individual and the social. It is the philosophy of a radically individualist ethos, as Foigny too seems to suggest.

to a closed monoculture such as the Southern Land. The view of Foigny as a deist and rationalist overlooked (forgivably, insofar as it was based on the 1692 edition) the fact that he debunks those ideals by portraying such a society and then exposing its delusions about its relationship with the world. For as Marin observes, formal logic is a utopia's referential signified—what it really aims to (de)construct.[46]

At the level of the individual, a related development concerns the logical inconsistency (as Suains sees it) of the notion of an afterlife. Sadeur gropes for a psychological explanation: this is not intended, he says, in any literal or physical sense but as a metaphor figuring the esteem or otherwise of the community one leaves behind. But Suains is unable to grasp the concept except in terms of metempsychosis, the transmigration of souls from one form of life to another (as, for example, in Hindu beliefs). After this Sadeur becomes more confident in his rejection of the Australian philosophy. He sees that perfect rationality, although a laudable goal in itself, is an impossible one because it seeks to transcend the limits imposed by space and time, by geography and history.

"To err is human," in other words. It is the distortion caused by relative isolation, falling short of a universal truth that might prevail if there were no such boundaries, that forms the field of difference in which human culture grows. To deny this fact by supposing that an "unbounded" situation already exists is to ignore humanity's past and to preempt what may be its future, but it is, in any case, to deny the reality of its present. "This nation," Sadeur concludes, "is capable of a great deal; reason

46. Marin (1984, 10). As noted, it used to thought that Foigny's utopia advocated a positive, deistic rationalism. But it was a calculated departure into pure rationality in order to question uncritical or optimistic assumptions about it. Leibacher-Ouvrard (1989, 24) observes that the brevity of Foigny's exposition of his language suggests that he knew what problems he would make for himself if he took it any further.

guides it and would make it incomparable if joined to faith, but this same reason that raises it so far above others in natural knowledge drags it down beneath all others in that it does not know its own salvation. You could say that its science serves only to blind it."

These materialists have no concept of the soul as a moral construct or a projection of personal identity. They are not really persons at all in that sense but units in an antlike society—psychic clones. Nor do the conditions of Australian life favor the formation of such a concept; there is neither difference within (arising from sexual binarity and kinship) nor difference without, arising from contiguity with other nations. To be totally human and transcend "bestial" parochialisms, they believe, it is necessary both to be hermaphroditic and to live in a single, unbounded state. They suppose themselves to have such absolute boundaries and assume similar boundaries between nature and culture or between life and death.

Their ethos is thus a "u-topia" in a more than literal (geographical) sense; it is an abstraction from reality in every way. An absolute boundary is tantamount to an absence of boundary; any real boundary is the site of an unresolved tension. This absolute of humanity is in effect—because "absolved" from difference, from the duality of an interior and exterior—an absence of humanity. A holocaust of violence finally exposes it as a death culture, completing a series of dialogues that revealed not only inconsistencies in the Australian ethos but the inevitability of rational inconsistency itself—what the Australians claim to have transcended in their cocoon world.

That proposition is set up only to be knocked down and critically dissected. As the work makes its *U*-turn and worldly reality invades the utopia, it is revealed as problematical and, finally, impossible. Having been carefully structured using numerological and other symbolism, it is just as systematically deconstructed. Foigny illustrates in this way a paradoxical truth about human society: that although in itself ideally closed and monocultural, it is in practice open to a world of travel, war, commerce, and cultural plurality. All nations resemble to an extent this Southern Land that imagines itself to have absolute boundaries and a fixed identity (but experiences history as their erosion). When that ideal becomes obsessive, when that erosion is too strenuously resisted, they inevitably experience the sort of violence that takes over in the later chapters of this story.

It was a point that subsequent political history would amply bear out and a timely one. For the modern opening of society through culture-contact was, in Foigny's day, rapidly leading to a "crisis of European consciousness" (Hazard 1953) from which would arise an age of Enlightenment and a dynamic new form of society. Parallel developments in the realm of ideas would later lead to the philosophical insights of Kant; by way, precisely, of a process of "neutralizing" abstraction such as is personified by Foigny's hermaphrodites.[47]

A more directly anthropological manifestation of the same effect would be Swift's Houyhnhnm satire in the fourth book of *Gulliver's Travels* (1726)—a reversion to animality.[48] The prospect had arisen of a secular basis for society, consistent with the new materialism and displacing its traditional basis in revealed (metaphysical) truth. The form such developments might take was still conjectural, but a familiar mold in which to cast it was the internal uniformity and equality that primitivists or satirists associated with savage society. Foigny, too, attempted in his way—with his "test-tube" society—to confront traditional social ideals with modern geopolitical realities.

47. The link between Kantian and utopian thought is discussed by Marin (1984, 19–22). Benrekassa (1980, 260), too, notes that the pre-scientific anthropology embodied in works such as Foigny's anticipated by a century the Kantian question, "What is man?"

48. As noted by Benrekassa (1980, 244–49).

Boundaries of the Physical

The Australians' ultimate undoing occurs, however, in a dimension that transcends even terraqueous communication. As a dichotomy emerges between the natural and the cultural, it becomes clear that the Australians' constant concern is to repress the former. Yet it returns with a vengeance in the air; the Urgs are their most feared enemies because they come and go in a medium that is totally foreign. Like death itself, they represent an "other" that no dialectician can encompass. They are an even purer manifestation of the physical than Fundian or European "half-men" or that other aquatic horror, fish, and are, therefore, more totally the nemesis of the Australians. With Sadeur's escape on the back of one, their significance is fully revealed; it becomes clear that the ground-air divide represents the ultimate boundary in this play of boundaries (a point again illustrated by modern military practices).

The air supplants the sea as a medium of communication and dissolution, this time representing a power the Australians can neither master nor, like Sadeur, negotiate with. Again, within the analogy set up between the sea and language, this ultimate power corresponds to writing—a power that "realizes" the primitive word, enabling it to endure in time and cross spatial frontiers. A power implicit, too, in cartographical and navigational skills such as those that bring European "sea monsters" to the Southern Land and implicit (or even explicit) in the real ethnographic processes that would be instrumental in dissolving the ethnic isolation of New World societies.[49]

Sadeur learns during this experience that "no man is an island." He returns to a world of compromise: a world torn by conflicts over truth and meaning, over woman's share in a "man's

---

49. Cf., for example, Lévi-Strauss (1968, chap. 18, "The Writing Lesson").

world," over territory and the social rights it confers. He accepts the tension of warring forces one inhabits, the claims of the flesh, and the claim ultimately made on the flesh. In the course of his adventures he becomes a master of media, initially of the physical kind (as the prophet of a new "transport culture") and, ultimately, of the discursive kind. His experiences make him a writer, his word becomes a testament. As such he achieves, ironically, what the Australians fruitlessly aspire to—transcendence of their mortality. After all his symbolic rebirths, he is reborn into philosophical wisdom and becomes a kind of messiah figure—as the recurrent parallels with the story of Christ suggested he might.

Like Christ, too, he is transmuted into a pure abstract concept, a written text. This is what the closure of his life leads to; and it also illustrates an aspect of travel fiction that put it in the mainstream of literary developments at the time. Personal memoirs were a major component of such writing and even tended to become a genre in their own right. The effect is prefigured when the young Sadeur, uprooted from his past and not knowing his true identity, receives it from a Jesuit priest in Lisbon in the form of a memoir.[50] From there he goes on to encounter a whole nation of such people, divorced from any organic relation with their pasts either as individuals or as a collectivity (their annals and origins myth, for example, are less a history in this sense than a parody of biblical myth). Here again, one recalls Arthus's hermaphrodites, who are forbidden to speak of their history.

In this way, the history of individuals is doubled by that of nations. The Australians' collective myth of autarchy mirrors the way they conceive of themselves as persons. It has a distinctly modern ring to it and anticipated the thrust of the ideological revolution about to overtake Europe, ushering in a world where

50. As pointed out by Racault (1991, VI:1).

direct experience would be mediated or supplanted by representation—given, in effect, as a text. Such was, in general, the project of "that *feigned* discovery of a *fictive* society that a utopia is," as Benrekassa puts it, noting too that "the utopia is a purely testamentary (form of) language, whose whole legacy is in the words of the testament."[51]

The closure of that double circle—a death that gives birth to a text—doubles the completion of Sadeur's utopian journey by transposing it onto a higher level of significance as a written text. The world, like the flesh, becomes the word, and so is preserved. As Sadeur finally succumbs to the sea in Livorno, his manuscript ("much stained by seawater") is given into the hands of the "editor" who, in effect, is a midwife in his final rebirth into posterity as a writer.[52]

This aspect may enable one, finally, to arrive at some conclusions about Foigny's intentions in the work. The general destiny of the physical that it elaborates—to become the word—seems to hold a universal message that in dying, one becomes a finished "text" in the minds of those one leaves behind (as Sadeur had tried to explain to Suains). Foigny's work was no less than an attempt to demystify the theological concept of afterlife, to recast it in psychological and sociological terms. It was a response to the relativizing effect of the New World experience on revealed religion, filling the void it had been cast into as a basis for practical social conduct.

His project involved a revision not only of the traditional conception of a personal god but also of its association with paternity. In the words of Georges Benrekassa (1980, 273), Foigny's hermaphrodite myth "joins orphic cosmogonies, and especially the ancient myth of the Phoenix, a double being that

51. Benrekassa (1980, 260, 245).

52. It may be significant that Sadeur's name, which Ronzeaud (1982a, 76) associates with the French *sauveur* (saviour), more closely resembles that of the *siddur* or Jewish prayer book.

fecundates and engenders itself, an *autopater* [self-fathering be-ing] and therefore eternal." He rooted the work in ancient Earth Mother ideas and drew on Hellenistic voyage utopias (see n. 31) that had similarly visited that radically different world of ideas from the archaic East: a concept of human existence that tran-scended territorial boundaries and the masculine practices of ideology and war based on them.

Foigny's thought reached back into prehistory but was also a long way ahead of his time. Like Sadeur, he would be resurrected through his word—after three hundred years. It can be seen how acutely he perceived modern trends in many areas of life yet how skeptical he was of them from his standpoint within a classical worldview. The little that is known about his life helps to explain why he had such strong views and how he arrived at this means of expressing them. In the end, he seems to telescope right into his creation.

The Southern Land, Known

Notice to the Reader

Man has no characteristic more natural than the desire to comprehend what he considers difficult and to penetrate what to many appears inaccessible. He is born with this passion and gives fresh proof of it with everything he undertakes. He even tries to climb into the heavens and, not content with reasoning and arguing about the nature of the stars, delves into the secrets of divinity. It is all the more astonishing, then, that for four or five hundred years the existence of an unknown southern land has been suggested without anyone so far having had the courage and the inclination to make it known.[1]

It is true that Magellan enjoyed for a while the glory of discovering it in 1520 in the name of "Terra del fuego," but the Dutch deprived

---

1. This takes the imaginary history back to 1176–1276: the time of the Crusades and of vague stirrings of real interest in Europe's exterior. Ancient cosmological traditions then acquired new prestige. The Macrobian hypothesis, for example, envisaged four continents separated by great ocean-rivers, corresponding to the Old World, Africa, North America, and the Southland. Reports of travelers such as Marco Polo also began to come in at that time. The 1692 version reduces the period mentioned to two hundred years, bringing the time in question to around 1476 (that of the Portuguese voyages down the west coast of Africa to open up a sea route to the East Indies).

him of that honor by proving that he only saw some islands to the south of America.[2] Some believe that the Frenchman Gonneville might deserve the honor because he, having fitted out a vessel at Honfleur, sailed on 12 June 1603 and arrived safely at the Cape of Good Hope, where he was driven by a violent storm into an unknown sea and finally onto the coast of the Southern Land. After staying there for six months he resolved to return to France and brought with him a young man whom he described as the son of a local king.[3]

That was his story, but because he gave no indications of the location or extent of the country, it cannot be judged for certain. Marco Polo, the Venetian, had done more a long time previously, if one is to believe his account. He discovered, opposite Greater Java, the province of Beach, which he described as full of riches; as well as the kingdom of Maletur, abounding in spices, the island of Petan with its aromatic trees, and another island that he called Little Java.[4] But the Dutch, who trade regularly in Greater

2. Magellan believed that the land he saw to the south of his straight was the southern continent. But the Dutchmen Jacob Le Maire and Willem Schouten proved in 1616 that it was an island by rounding Cape Horn farther to the south.

3. This voyage was referred to by Jean Paulmier, canon of St. Paul de Lisieux and a descendant of Essomerik (the man brought back by Binot Paulmier de Gonneville, and baptized in his name), in a tract proposing a missionary expedition to the land of his ancestor: *Mémoires touchant l'établissement d'une mission chrestienne dans le troisième monde autrement appelé la Terre Australe . . .* (Paris: Cramoisy, 1663). The date he gave was 1503; that of 1603 was a mistake on the part of Thévenot, who would be branded *cet âne* (that ass) by a later advocate of French activity in the austral regions, Charles De Brosses, for his slip (considerable importance being attached to this supposed evidence of French priority there). The Gonneville story is now thought to refer to a voyage to Brazil; see Friedrich (1967a, 220) and, in general, Fausett 1993, chap. 1.

4. "Java" was a term loosely applied to major land masses in the region in early times. The other names mentioned are thought to be distortions of local names ("Maletur" is Malaya, and "Beach" corresponds to Indochina). These places were on the Chinese trading circuit, the source of Polo's information.

Java, assure us that this whole discovery was only that of a few islands and not of the Great Southern Land. This conclusion seems all the more likely in that Fernandes Gallego, having crossed the vast sea between the Strait of Magellan and the Moluccas, reported finding such a large chain of islands that he counted 1,070 of them.[5]

All these claims and counterclaims involving famous people lend weight to Ranty's proposition in the introduction to his *Cosmographie* that "no one has as yet known what the Southern Land is, nor even whether it is inhabited."[6] Indeed, it must be admitted when comparing the account of the Portuguese Fernandez Quirós with the one to follow here that if anyone deserves this honor it is he, rather than any of his predecessors.

We read in this eighth *Requeste* to his Catholic Majesty that in the course of his discoveries of 1610,[7] he saw lands of the austral continent surpassing those of Spain in fertility where the inhabitants were numerous and of a carefree, amiable disposition. They were respectful and demure in manner, bigger and taller of body than we are, healthy and long-lived, and remarkably skilled at a variety of tasks having to do, in particular, with cultivation, boat building, and textiles. Luis Paez de Torres was admiral of the same fleet, and he confirmed Quirós's report to the Spanish ministry, adding that these lands were so healthy and so agreeable to man's temperament that one could sleep out in the open

---

5. Gallego, a pilot (navigator) on Mendaña's 1567 Pacific expedition during which the Solomon Islands were discovered, was the first to claim to have searched actively for the southern land. His account was published in Herrera's *Historia general* (Madrid, 1601–1615). Information from Gallego and his fellow pilot Gamboa was a major source for the maps of Ortelius and others of the later sixteenth century that showed the imaginary southern continent.

6. Foigny's geographical information was in part derived from two "Introductions to Cosmography" by Baron Gaston Jean-Baptiste de Renty or Ranty (Paris, 1645 and 1657).

7. Cf. introduction, p. xxx and, in general, Markham 1904.

quite safely; that he and his troops had slept with equal pleasure by day or night; that the fruits there were so fine and nourishing that they alone sufficed as food; that a liquor more pleasant than our wines was drunk there; that the use of clothes was unknown, and that the natural sciences were held in great esteem. Such were, in short, the reports of these two characters so deserving of glorious memory; and what follows will make it apparent that, if they did not actually travel through those vast lands, at least they came very close to them.[8] Their brush, however, is light of touch: it serves only to arouse our curiosity because they neglect to paint in any details.

The illumination of these shadows had to await the reign of Louis the Redoubtable and the Triumphant, so that if two continents were not a sufficient conquest for him, he could yet know of a third, better situated and incomparably better arranged than the others.[9] There might, perhaps, be some dispute about the nation to which we owe this rich illumination: Spain will, no doubt, claim the honor because our author was educated in Portugal.[10] But because the tree is known by the fruit, and his father and mother were French, we can be certain that this claim is rightfully France's.

Indeed, such rare and brilliant revelations as he makes could have no other origin than this nation that bursts ever more brilliantly upon the world. Certainly, if I had not happened to be at Livorno in 1661 as he was disembarking, his memoirs would have fallen into foreign hands, which would, no doubt, have

8. Here Foigny plays on the skepticism with which the traveler's tale had traditionally been received, preparing in this way his own slide from historical fact into a realm of ambiguous truth. A grain of ethnographic truth can, for example, be seen in the descriptions of Quirós and Torres (as in those of Columbus and other early navigators).

9. A satirical reference to Louis XIV's aggressive foreign policies, as was common in utopias of the time.

10. Portugal had been under Spanish rule since 1580.

robbed him of this glory. But the good fortune that was always his and a spirit of generosity that refuses to tolerate such injustice infallibly led me to him to prevent this from happening.

I was at the docks when the vessel that brought him from Madagascar anchored. The disembarkation was somewhat hurried, as is usual after such long voyages, with the result that our author, weakened no doubt by the trials of a voyage of three or four thousand leagues,[11] slipped off the gangplank and fell into the water with a small suitcase he was carrying. The fellow was tragically dying in port, without anyone lifting a finger to save him. I took pity and ran over and managed to reach down a pole, which saved him from drowning. Once out of the water he expressed his gratitude—as much by signs as by words—giving me to understand that he was totally destitute but would appreciate the chance to tell me his story. His kindness of face and gentleness of manner made an impression on me and, although a foreigner, I took him to my lodgings and treated him as a Christian should.

Scarcely had he changed his clothes and had something to eat, when two sailors approached me and asked for fifteen pistoles, the cost of his fare and board from Madagascar. I tried to talk my way out of it but got nowhere and went to see the ship's captain. He received me politely, being himself French and sympathetic toward the poor traveler who had, it appeared, considerably enlightened him about the Southern Land during the voyage.

On returning to my lodgings I found the fellow bathed in tears and did all I could to console him. He repeated several times that he believed I was his angel and that God had sent me to bear witness to his story. I persuaded him to unburden himself right away, and he began relating his adventures with a frankness I admired. He spoke for nearly two whole hours in Latin, and I enjoyed listening to him so much that I scarcely noticed the time

---

11. Nine thousand to twelve thousand nautical miles.

passing. Seeing, however, that he was growing tired—and placing his health above my curiosity—I asked him to break off his story. "I wish I could finish now," he said, "what I want to tell you. I do not think we will have another chance. I feel that at long last I have come to the end of my path, and in truth I find it has been a long and difficult one." I felt his pulse and noticed it was very irregular, which caused me to stop him from talking any further and put him to bed.

The following day I realized that he was really ill and sent for the doctor. He prescribed a bleeding, which the old man refused, saying that it was a useless remedy and that he was near the end in any case. His fever worsened that evening, and he made his Christian preparations for the great voyage into eternity. On the following day, which was the 25th of March, the Day of the Incarnation of the Son of God, he called me around three o'clock in the morning and told me he was about to leave this world. He thanked me affectionately for my care and asked me to open his suitcase. In it I found a kind of book, a bundle of pages about one foot long, six fingers wide, and two thick; it was a collection of his adventures written in Latin, partly right in the Southern Land and partly at Madagascar. As well there were four small scrolls, each two and one-half yards long and one foot wide, very delicately worked, which would have retained their luster had the seawater not faded it. This he graciously offered me in the presence of our Host, begging me at the same time to take the trouble to bury him decently. Scarcely had he finished when he seized my hand with a grip that told me he was breathing his last.

It did not take long for the local governor to find out that a foreigner had died leaving some rare and precious property. I was obliged to take it to him, and, because he threatened to confiscate it "for his Highness," I gave him all of it except the book, which I kept to pay for the funeral expenses.

I read the book, although with great difficulty because of its staining by seawater. I have kept it for fifteen years as an inestimable treasure and have at last decided to publish it because, in revealing the workings of divine wisdom, it obliges us to admire the latter's influence. It shows up the hypocrisy of many who profess to be Christians endowed with special grace but who live worse than beasts; whereas a pagan people, illuminated only by natural wisdom, proves to be even more virtuous than Protestants. I am quite aware that those who measure the divine from within the limits of their own imagination will see the work only as a fiction, made to entertain, but that does not seem a sufficient reason to withhold truths that might enlighten the whole of Europe.

The merest tincture of reason suffices to persuade one that, because nothing in this story is impossible, one should at least suspend judgment as to what might be possible or real. In any case, I have reproduced our Author's text as closely as possible, taking out only some purely philosophical matters to keep the story pure and entertaining. It is not that I would presume to keep these from the public, but I thought that my making them into a separate treatise I might be able to give a better idea of the great enlightenment the Australians enjoy in comparison to the darkness that envelops our minds.[12]

---

12. Most of these preliminaries, and all beyond the mention of Quirós, were omitted from the 1692 version, despite their evident importance in situating the story historically, geographically, and philosophically. The philosophical section was reduced to three sentences, indicating that the narrative had hitherto been unavailable because it was "locked in the cabinet of a great minister." Foigny's ploy of "novelizing" the problem of truth by referring to the discovery of Australia was largely lost in the process.

CHAPTER ONE

Sadeur's Birth and Education

I find I am unable to reflect on all the adventures of my life without admiring in them the workings of divine providence, and feel that I should gather them all together and set out their more remarkable aspects. Even though they are unlikely to edify my countrymen (as I see little prospect of returning), it seems worthwhile to put them down in writing for my own satisfaction so as to be able to go over them more often in my memory and pay constant homage to my adorable Guide.

While in the Villa Franca household during my youth in Portugal, I received a memoir from a Jesuit Father in Lisbon containing the following details of my early life. My father was Jaques Sadeur and my mother, Guillemette Ottin,[1] both of them from Chatillon-sur-Bar in the district of Rethel in Champagne, a province of France. My father knew many secrets of mathematics, rather through the instruction of nature than that of any master. He excelled in particular in inventions that facilitated the bearing of heavy burdens. A Mr. de Vanre, who held a

1. The 1692 edition has "Itin." Such comparisons will be cited as "1692: . . . " Archaic spellings such as "Jaques" are preserved in the text.

position of some importance in the navy, met him and offered him posts at Bordeau[x] and then in the West Indies, seducing my father with what he considered were sufficient promises.

My mother accompanied him on the voyage but pressed him to return after nine or ten months at Port Royal and having embarked on 25 April 1603,[2] she gave birth to me a fortnight later. Mr. de Sare, the ship's captain, wanted to be my godfather, and it was deemed appropriate to name me Nicholas because I was born on the high seas where that saint is so often invoked. Thus I was conceived in America and born upon the ocean, a too-telling presage of what I would one day become.[3] The voyage was safe throughout the parts considered dangerous, but then within sight of the coast of Aquitaine a sudden storm hit the ship, throwing her furiously onto the Spanish coast close to Cape Finisterre[4] in the province of Gallaecia. She was wrecked, with the loss of my parents.

The memoir related how my mother, seeing the ship taking water on all sides, took me from my cot and kissed me with the greatest tenderness, saying through her tears, "Dear child, I have borne you on the ocean wave only to see you engulfed straight-away by the same waters; at least I shall have the consolation of dying with you!" She had not finished bemoaning our fate when a still more violent wave broke over the ship, carrying her away from my father. In this perilous moment everyone looked out for

2. Cf. "Notice to the Reader," n. 3. Port Royal was the French establishment on the Bay of Fundy in Canada.

3. 1692: "of the misfortunes that would buffet me throughout my life." This change loses the sense of the original, which (as outlined in my introduction) presages Sadeur's destiny to become a text, transmuted from a physical existence into an abstract, written one.

4. *Fine terrae* (land's end) in the original text; its metaphorical significance is obscured in the 1692 version, which has the more prosaic "Finisterre." Foigny's land-sea imagery becomes clearer as the work progresses.

their own survival; except for my parents who, putting mine ahead of their own, exposed themselves to certain death in trying to save me. My mother's devotion was such that she did not abandon me and eventually drowned through constantly holding me up out of the water. My father's courage was just as remarkable because he, instead of making for the shore like the others, came to us in our desparate plight, taking hold of my mother who was still holding me up and pulling us to shore. After laying us on the sand he himself, either through exhaustion or because he believed us both dead, fainted with me in his arms.

Although the other passengers were in similar straits, there was not one who was not impressed by this spectacle; several even came to our help. Realizing that I was still alive, they took me from my father's arms and set me beside the fire that the compassionate local inhabitants had lit. No sign of life could be got out of my mother, and it was decided, after warming her beside the fire for a time, that nothing could be done except bury her.

Those who had known my father deplored his loss with cries that drew tears from the local people. "What a good man!" some said. "Such a generous soul, that he should perish in saving his family's life." "Ah," said others, "has there ever been such a tragedy? A mother sacrificing herself for her child, a father sacrificing himself for the mother, and all that courage leaving nothing but dead bodies." Perhaps because of this commotion, the good man then came to his senses. He slowly opened his eyes and was heard to ask in a faint voice, "Where are you, dear friend?" This utterance took the group by surprise, and because they were struck dumb he added, "Well, then, let us all die together." These were his last words before he closed his eyes to this life. He is supposed to have distinguished himself in a number of ways during the voyage, but in this extremity he drew everyone's admiration.

Just as he was breathing his last, I started up with loud signs of life, and I am told that some of the company could not help regarding my survival as a kind of affront. "You poor leftover," they said, "what will become of you? What fortune can life bring you now that you have been the death of those who gave you life?" Some of them believed that I could not survive because my father had called for me while dying, but this was mere superstition. I was just beginning a career of tragedy that has already lasted fifty-five years and has been filled with so many and such strange catastrophes that I would scarcely be believed even if I were able to recount them all.

The warmth of the fire gave me back enough strength to complain, crying so lustily that it was clear that I was out of the clutches of death. One of the locals knew enough French to understand the situation, and his memory of the only son he had lost some time before—whom I resembled in a certain way—caused him to offer to adopt me. It was pointed out to Mr. de Sare that this was a very favorable opportunity: that refusing it would only burden himself and put me in further danger. He therefore handed me over, more out of necessity than any other consider-ation. The man took me in right away in place of his lost son, and his wife, having heard of all that had happened, kissed me and received me with the utmost tenderness.

Mr. de Sare and his officers, realizing that they were not far from St. Jaques,[5] decided to go there. They were fortunate enough to find some respectable merchants[6] and fitted them-selves out to return to Oléron. Once home the captain told of the shipwreck and all that he had been through. But his wife did not think much of it at the time, being full of the joy of her husband's deliverance from such a long and ill-fated voyage. This engaged the affections she was later to bestow on me. Some time later she asked her husband to retell the story and could not help admiring

5. Santiago de Compostela, the site of an old shrine to St. James believed to contain relics of his body.

6. *Des marchands de connoissance,* which could also be read as "sellers of knowledge."

the conjugal and parental love that had led my mother and father to a voluntary death.[7] But instead of arousing her indignation, my wretched person inspired in her such affection—especially when she learned that her husband was my godfather—that she nagged him into finding the means of abducting me.

Accordingly, he set sail again about twenty-two months after his return, and two weeks later arrived at Camarinas where he found me a thriving child of thirty months, secure in the love of the mother and father whom I now took to be my real parents. When he made known the reason for his visit and his intention of paying them for the time they had looked after me, they were highly offended and refused to let me go. Mr. de Sare claimed his right as godparent, whereas the Spaniards insisted that he had formerly made a gift of me. The case was thrashed out before the court of Camarinas, which decided in favor of my adoptive parents; whereupon Mr. de Sare, more a soldier than a man of letters, decided to seize me and make off with the wind, which was favorable at that moment, rather than be thwarted in his designs. He burst into the house with a valet and, finding only a servant in charge of me, took me in his arms and made for his ship, which was ready to sail.

Fear, mingled with the stress of my protests, soon reduced me to a faint and caused me a nearly fatal fever. My adoptive father, justifiably irate at this coup, rushed down to the port with some friends. Because we were by then beyond attack, they fired a cannon at us. This, however, drew a volley from a Portuguese ship passing on its way south, which proved fatal for us when one of their balls came through our bulwarks and sank the vessel—not without regret on their part at causing the death of those who, as far as they knew, were innocent parties caught in the middle. Those on shore fled when they saw the accident, while the Portuguese sent two boats to rescue the drowning crew.

---

7. This will later become a central theme. See chap. 7.

Their efforts managed to save only a valet able to swim better than the others and myself, floating in my straw-filled cot.[8] I hesitate to relate what one can surely not read without considering me worse than a serpent for it seems that I live only to cause the death of those involved with me. The Portuguese, fearing reprisal for this unprovoked attack, headed for the high seas. Finding me still alive although very thirsty, they gave me into the care of a matron on board, who was very anxious to look after me until she discovered that I was of both sexes—I mean, a hermaphrodite. When she discovered this, the woman was seized with such aversion that she could not even stand the sight of me, and because my fever was now rising considerably I would certainly have died if Mr. de Sare's valet had not taken care of me.

Indeed, it might seem that God had preserved him only to relieve my plight, if I had been able to recompense him in some way. When we arrived at Leiria,[9] he took me from door to door, recommending me for adoption as if I had been his own child. Meanwhile, the Portuguese captain, glad to be rid of us, sailed away without his knowing. The valet, on hearing that the great poorhouse in Lisbon would be able to offer more assistance than Leiria, decided to take me there. As a Frenchman he was quite welcome;[10] but no sooner had we arrived than a mortal fever took hold of him, and he died seven days later in the arms of the Jesuit who, as I said, was to pass on these details to me fifteen years later in his memoir. As he died, the poor fellow, instead of regretting his misfortune and blaming me for it, continued commending me to those helping him, even more emphatically than if I had belonged to him.

The Jesuits, on learning of all the evils that had befallen me till then, consulted gravely among themselves as to what should

8. A "ridiculous Moses," as Benrekassa (1980, 267) puts it.
9. A village north of Lisbon.
10. That is, as an ally of Spanish-occupied Portugal.

become of me, and it was decided that my inclinations should be studied carefully before any decision was made. By the time I was five, however, they knew enough to conclude that I was not a lost cause and that the disorders of my early life should be attributed to circumstance rather than to my own nature. They noticed my leanings toward the religious life and that my mind held considerable promise if cultivated. When I was eight they introduced me to the Countess of Villa Franca, having told her of my early misfortunes. This lady, who compares favorably with even the most illustrious of her predecessors, took me in with such kindness that she arranged for me to be treated and educated as an equal with her son, the young count, then aged nine. Although I wore their colors[11] for eight years, I had no other obligations than to accompany him in his studies, and I learned with him Latin, Greek, French, Italian, and the principles of African,[12] as well as geometry, geography, philosophy, chronology, and Spanish history. The countess showed the same affection toward me as to her own family, and on learning how much I contributed to her son's progress, she suggested that I put aside the colors and take up philosophy.

Some time after doing so I was asked to second the Count in his examination at the University of Coimbra,[13] where I would deliver a speech in his honor and open the debate. For more than a fortnight before our departure I was so agitated and emotionally upset that my health suffered visibly. Sometimes my blood would run cold, as if I were about to be tortured, and my heart would pound as if I were standing on a cliff-top. At other times I was seen to alternately pale and blush. The worst of all this was that everyone thought I was merely suffering from stage fright brought on by fear of the coming public appearance. All I can say

11. That is, as a valet.
12. "African" presumably means here Arabic.
13. In central Portugal. The university was founded in 1306.

about the nightmares and specters of all kinds that engulfed me at this time is that once I knew of the Count's decision to go by sea, all that I had been told of the early misfortunes that had befallen me on the sea crowded into my mind, so that I could not distinguish between my embarking with him and his inevitable doom.

I therefore arranged permission to make the journey by land with part of his entourage. But as in "the best-laid plans of mice and men," my seeking to avoid the evil that threatened me was what made it inevitable. I made such a fuss about my departure that I appeared ridiculous, and the Countess regarded as effeminate my weeping at her feet. The Count, who was like a brother to me, asked, "Sadeur, do you want to leave us? You are no longer yourself; what is it that torments you? I think you must be nursing some design of your own; a simple case of stage fright could scarcely make you lose your reason." "Sire," I replied, "if God brings me back I shall explain then this attack of weakness; but in the meantime, I beg you to suspend your judgment." The young aristocrat was so taken aback by this response that he insisted that I either travel with him or not make the journey at all. To this I replied, "As for the journey itself, your honor is at stake, and I will either make it or else die in the attempt; but as far as accompanying you by sea is concerned, although I would gladly risk it if only my own life were at stake, I will disobey you at whatever cost rather than put yours in danger." These words, together with his affection for me, reduced him to silence, and we parted company the following day.

Philip II of Castile, having taken possession of Portugal in 1581, had elevated a number of families to positions of power to underpin his position there, among which was the House of Villa Franca. But this had not been done without incurring the jealousy of a number of others who believed themselves more deserving of the honor, and among these was the House of Braganza. Because it is easier to conquer lands than hearts, many

Portuguese remained faithful to the Braganzas, whose ambition was to shake off the Catalan yoke and install their duke on the throne. Even though the country was securely under the thumb of the kings of Spain, local revolts were still very frequent, and the coasts harbored pirates who vented their hatred of Spanish domination in all their dealings.

Thus it was that the Count's departure on 15 May 1623 was common knowledge, and two Braganza vessels were dispatched to kidnap him. They attacked the two escort vessels off Tomar; but these repulsed the attack so strongly that it was scattered, to the Count's glory. I was following behind with the land party and knew nothing of the engagement until these vicious enemies, having landed a party of thirty musketeers, ambushed us and killed a page, two valets, and my horse. The others, unable to defend themselves, fled, and these inhuman beasts, worse than flesh-crazed wolves,[14] dragged me brusquely aboard their vessel and headed to sea.

14. These details, the beginning of a complex nature-culture leitmotiv, were omitted from the 1692 version.

CHAPTER TWO

Sadeur's Voyage to the Kingdom of Congo

It is certainly true that man proposes, but God disposes. I had believed that in traveling by land I would avoid the dangers of the sea; but the sea, so to speak, came to get me on the land, dragging me back into all the miseries that I had sought to escape from. The pirates had not long been at sea when the latter rose into such a violent storm that the pilots despaired of surviving it. The vessel's mast broke, the rudder went, and she began to take water everywhere. We were tossed about at the mercy of the waves for twenty-four hours, working six great pumps day and night until, with the crew exhausted, the water at last gained the upper hand and sank the ship. I found myself at the time—I cannot imagine why—near the door of the captain's cabin, which broke free and began to float away. To avoid drowning I latched onto it, as much by natural impulse as by any reasoning or inspiration. I do not know how long I remained like that because I was in such a state of shock that I had no powers of judgment. I only know that, thanks to the moonlight, I was spotted by a ship sailing south, which sent a boat to investigate what I might be. Finding that I was a dying man, they took me aboard.

I had only just recovered my senses when I was recognized as having been in Lisbon and in the Villa Franca household, and the captain ordered that particular care be taken of me because he was greatly obliged to that illustrious family. Before long I had fully regained my health; and I then pleaded with my rescuers to put me ashore, relating the series of betrayals that I had caused at sea and sparing no effort to make them realize that that element was extremely fatal to me. But the more I tried to convince them, the more ridiculous I appeared in their eyes. In the end I realized that I should simply abandon myself to divine Providence and its plans for me without persisting any further. The captain said that his obligation toward the house I had been in was such that he must hold me until he could hand me back personally to the Countess and that he expected this occasion to be more fortunate than all his other fortunes on the voyage.

I learned that this was a Portuguese fleet of four vessels en route to trade in the East Indies, and when its first secretary fell ill, I was invited to take his place. The wind was so favorable that the crew insisted I had brought good fortune, not bad, to their undertaking. We arrived hale and hearty at the equator on 15 July and at the Kingdom of Congo on the 1st of September, anchoring at Maninga on the 6th. Our only problem was the secretary's illness, which was steadily worsening, and the doctor advised that he be rested ashore because there was no prospect of his recovering at sea. The captains and pilots agreed, furthermore, that the rounding of the Cape of Good Hope should be delayed until after the approaching equinox, so it was decided to remain at Maninga until December for both the sick man's sake and ours.

We encountered three Portuguese there, who knew the local language and told of such wonders in that kingdom that we were struck with admiration.[1] It was truly an earthly paradise that

1. This episode is the first of the symmetrical halfway houses mentioned in the introduction. Maninga is identified by Ronzeaud (1990, 36)

they described, filled with all that humans could desire for their health and pleasure. There was no need to cultivate the earth— by contrast with the poverty of ours, so overworked and eroded by wind and extremes of weather. My natural curiosity to investigate nature's secrets was aroused on listening to these men, and I decided to go and see for myself what otherwise was only hearsay. Here is a summary of what I saw.

The country is only half as densely populated as Portugal; I am not sure whether this should be attributed to their marked lack of interest in reproducing or to the difficulties of doing so. The men go entirely naked, although in recent years some have begun to imitate the European habit of covering that which (we are told) is shameful. Everywhere the abundance of the land makes them vague, lazy, simple, and stupid. After studying them for a while, I was forced to conclude that human nature grows lazy when it lacks nothing, that idleness makes it dull and insensitive. Man, it seemed to me, must exercise and extend himself, must aspire, unless he wants to turn to stone; the moment he loses his ambition he becomes paralyzed. The land hereabouts, especially between the Zaire and Cariza rivers, yields an abundance of produce without needing to be cultivated. And these fruits are so delicate and nourishing that they fully satisfy and sustain those who live on them.[2] Even the spring waters have a certain sweetness and succulence about them. We stayed there for a considerable time without spending anything, partly because the locals despised money and partly because the countryside supplied all our needs. Houses are of so little importance in this country that little time is spent in them. The nights are so

---

as Matinga, a port on the "Congo River" on a map in De Bry (1624), thought to be present-day Cabinda (an Angolan enclave in Zaire). Zaire is an old name for the Congo, now rehabilitated; and the Cariza and Cuama rivers mentioned further on (ibid., 37, 45) may be the Coanza and Zambezi reported (after Lopez) in De Bry.

2. The Australians' magic fruit, *Balf,* is prefigured here.

mild that they prefer to sleep out in the open; they scarcely know what a bed is, apart from the mattresses provided for invalids; the rest sleep right on the ground.

All this gave me the impression of a people who, with no work to do, live quite naturally in a state of idleness that leaves them dull, forgetful, sleepy, casual, and apathetic—because perfection requires exercise, work, and effort. It must be admitted that happiness is far from consisting of the possession of whatever one desires (however worthy a desire that may be) and that he who no longer desires anything in this world becomes stupid and no longer deserves to live because he is then incapable of action.

The captain allowed myself and three companions to travel up the Zaire as far as the lake of that name; and even if I were able to relate all the adventures and pleasures of that voyage, I would scarcely be believed. Here are a few of the more remarkable as I recall them.

We arrived at the lake after twenty-four days and spent ten days going around it and a further twenty returning to the fleet. The Zaire River is not swift; and because we had four strong rowers, we could easily cover fifteen to twenty-eight leagues[3] in one day. However, we never did more than eight on the way upstream, from which I concluded that the geographers' maps were notably inaccurate in locating Lake Zaire three hundred-odd leagues from the sea. What made our daily distances so short was the multitude of curiosities constantly before our eyes: fruits, flowers, fish, and animals. We scarcely encountered any spot in vast prairies sixty to eighty leagues long that was not bedecked with a marvelous carpet of flowers that would be considered choice in the richest gardens of Europe. I could not bear to see them trampled underfoot, yet their vast quantity made them of no more value than our field daisies.

3. Fifty or sixty miles.

Almost every tree was a fruit tree, bearing produce beyond comparison with the fruits we know. And nature has so well fitted them to the reach of the inhabitants that they can be picked easily and safely. Indeed, we lived entirely at her expense and were so well satisfied that we desired nothing more. Our pilot, Sebastian de Lez,[4] a man of great experience, responded to our expressions of surprise that one would go all the way to the Indies for delicacies and curiosities that did not compare to these by saying that these fruits were like cooked and seasoned meats— they kept their true flavor only for about four days. His words made me try an experiment, and I found that they indeed did not keep for long without spoiling. One certainly had the impression when eating them that they were perfectly cooked and digestible, by contrast with our foods, which always do as much harm as good and cause at least as much bitterness in the gut as sweetness in the mouth. The fruits of the Manicongo keep because of their rawness, which resists the heat of the place, whereas if they are cooked they go off straightaway. Nature has, moreover, provided a constant supply of ripe fruit; the trees are always laden with blossoms, buds, and fruit in various stages of ripeness.

Among the great quantity of fish I saw from the Zaire, two species especially interested me. One I would call Amphibions because in some ways they resemble dogs or foxes in the way they are able to leave the water and leap about on it, except that their paws are splayed like a duck's feet and their front legs two or three times shorter than their hind legs. They are so attracted to man that they will seek him and offer themselves like so many victims.[5] Sometimes they even leap right into boats and approach

4. The name of one of Quirós's officers and presumably not, therefore, a reference to Foigny's contemporary, Denis Vairasse d'Alais, the author of the *History of the Sevarites*.

5. Compare to a real account of paradisiac events at Réunion Island published in 1646 by Bontekoe (1929, 29–32).

the occupants to caress them in the manner of dogs. I saw this happen with my own eyes and was annoyed when a rower killed one in front of me. The locals call them "Cadseick," and their flesh is somewhat like our Spanish otter.

Another species of fish that I admired could fly; they might be named "sea peacock" although they are much finer and more brightly colored than our land variety. They rarely swim at the bottom of the water and are nearly always to be seen at the surface. Their feathers resemble true fish scales but in a delightful range of green, blue, yellow, and red hues. The ones I saw out of the water looked like large eagles with wings each spanning at least five or six feet. They gave the distinct impression of showing off, the way they frolicked about the boat, posing for those watching or twisting and turning in the air with their dazzling tails.

The riverbanks were home to many kinds of animals of which the most common and charming resembled the sheep raised around Leiria, except that these came in almost every color: I mean reds, greens, yellows, and a blue so striking that our purple of the best-prepared silk could not match it. I inquired as to why there was no trade in such brilliant luxuries and was told that this natural color vanished with the life of the animals.

Having arrived at the lake, we spent ten days exploring it and found its length to be about sixty leagues, its width about forty. We saw the beginning of the Niger, which is broad, handsome, and deep enough for a ship although it soon loses itself in the mountains of Benin. We stopped at the Nile, which is here no less imposing than the Niger, so that if it continues with the same dimensions for three hundred leagues or more, there is no doubt that it must reach right to the Mediterranean and would, therefore, greatly facilitate communication between the two seas via this place.

I inquired diligently as to the whereabouts of the Cocodrilles [crocodiles] that natural historians suppose to be abundant in these regions. But no one even knew what I was talking about, which made me suspect that these were merely stories hatched to frighten the simpleminded and to provide handy imagery for the rhetoric of politicians. If it is true that "travelers may lie by authority,"[6] it is even truer that they take advantage of this license to the extent of passing off almost nothing but fictions. The reason for this is that one often makes long passages with only brief stops in ports where tedium and all the petty irritations of travel force one to seek some relief. Moreover, because we are convinced that we must bring back novelties from a far destination, the more subtle the mind, the more it will invent them. And because there is no one to contradict them, such inventions are received with pleasure and hastily spread around as truths that it would be presumptuous to reject out of hand.

We next went to a small island in the middle of the lake belonging to the king of Zassaler, who also calls himself "King of the Lake." The locals call it Zasfla,[7] and the king has a fortress there that is greatly respected in these parts although it is not great by European standards. However, it was the island's interior that most drew our admiration; one could scarcely desire more than a few drafts of its heady aromatic scents. The fruits there were so fine, delicate, and abundant, that their beauty and their quantity actually became bothersome. But what was above all amazing and unheard-of was a spring that we found, the waters of which were even more fortifying than our Spanish wine.

We speculated at length about where such an agreeable liquor could come from and concluded that, because everything on the surface of this land was balmy, its interior must be likewise and that if there were bitter springs, reason dictated that there must also be sweet ones. We drank with a

6. As proclaimed by the second-century A.D. Greek satirist Lucian, who greatly influenced the imaginary voyage tradition.

7. Lake Victoria, shown on Ortelius's map as "Zaflan" (Ronzeaud 1990, 44).

pleasure I cannot describe, and one of us was just saying how he wished he could set up house there, when a local hastened to tell us that these waters were poisonous if drunk to excess. It did not take long for us to realize the truth of his words, for we became so sleepy that we had lie down where we were and were asleep for more than fifteen hours. But this slumber had no ill effects, and we got up just as fit as we had been before, if not more so. Some attributed this long rest to the excess of strong aromas that had filled our heads, others to the delicious drink that we had taken.

Leaving this island, we wanted to get to the source of the Cuama River, which we entered and found to be narrow and incapable of admitting any vessel. Shortly afterward we discovered the sources of the lake in the more than two hundred streams we counted rising in the mountains facing south, called by the Spanish "Mountains of the Moon" because Vasco da Gama, rounding the Cape of Good Hope in 1497 en route to the East Indies, noticed that the moon seemed to touch their peaks as it shone from behind them. The locals call them the "Ors," or Water Mountains, because of the abundant waters flowing from them. Those who confuse the Zembra River with the Zaire base their view on very inaccurate reports. We were told that it was on the other side of these mountains, at least fifty leagues away from the Zaire.

Most historians attribute a great variety of monsters to these regions, on no better authority than that of travelers' tales. All our investigations revealed only the origin of a neighboring people called Kaffirs by the Europeans or Tordi by the locals. We learned that a man of this area, having raised a pet tigress, became so familiar with the creature that he loved it carnally, committing the "great crime" with it. Out of this union was born a man-monster, the ancestor of these people who to this day cannot be humanized. Invincible proof of this story is provided by their faces and feet, which are very tiger-like; even their bodies are not without occasional markings similar to those of the tiger.[8]

We returned via the Cariza River and spent twenty days over the trip, savoring the same pleasures that we had enjoyed on the Zaire although what had previously enraptured us had by now become familiar and less exciting.

8. According to a real such legend, the Dahomey royal family of Abomey descended from a woman and a panther (Le Hérissé 1911). Sources for such ethnographic fantasy could, as noted, be found in De Bry, Bergeron, Renty, Thévenot, and others.

CHAPTER THREE

The Events Leading Sadeur
to the Southern Land

As soon as we returned the ship sailed with as fair a wind and sea as we could have wished for. In eight days we arrived at the Cape of Good Hope where we did not linger for fear of losing the good weather, so rare in those parts. Then within sight of the port of Annanbolo on the island of Madagascar, we were totally becalmed for more than forty-six hours, after which an easterly got up that blew so furiously against the sea current that it broke all our rigging and drove us more than one thousand leagues to the west. Some islands were seen to starboard, north of us, and taken to be those called the Trinity; and it was onto one of them that we were driven. The ship broke in two; and we were suddenly all, pilots, captains, and sailors alike, thrown at the mercy of the most pitiless of the elements.

I will never know what became of the other ships nor of my companions because it was a very dark night and I could think only of saving myself. My previous shipwrecks had given me experience and confidence in such circumstances; I had made ready a handy plank and whatever else I could for my survival, in spite of my great indifference to death when not in its clutches.

I floated for several hours on my plank, tossed about in a way I can only recall with a shudder: at times the violence of the waves dragged me under; at other times it rolled me over and over. I was unable to endure this treatment for long and passed out, after which I do not know what became of me nor what force preserved my life. All I remember is that on coming to and opening my eyes I found the sea calm and saw an island nearby. I noticed my hands were gripping my plank so tightly that I could scarcely let go; indeed, I have been unable to straighten my fingers ever since. The sight of this island gave me new strength, and on reaching its shore I dragged myself under a tree. But it was with more regret than relief at still being alive because I now faced a slow, languishing death.

Under this tree I found two fruits[1] of the size and almost the color of pomegranates, but which proved more delicate, more substantial, and more nourishing. When I had eaten the first, I felt fortified, and on eating the second, I was seized with a new vigor. But because I had suffered so much and could scarcely stand up, I lay down and fell into a deep sleep that lasted for twenty-four hours. After this I awoke feeling refreshed, with my clothes dried out and a hot sun in my face filling me with fresh hope. I found two more fruits and ate them, and then set about calculating the sun's elevation. I worked out that I must be in about 33 degrees of southerly latitude although I could have no idea at what longitude.[2]

After resting some more, I decided to venture into the island's interior and find out what inhabitants it might have. I

1. Probably a metaphor referring to the maternal breast, the whole ordeal being a symbolic rebirth.

2. A major problem in navigation and hydrography at the time, the calculation of longitude contributed much to the mystique and intrigue that became associated with the "great austral unknown."

actually saw what appeared to be tracks, but they led into thick undergrowth that could only be penetrated by doubling oneself up, which made me wonder. Finding a tree taller than the rest, I thought I should climb it and scan the countryside around. But as I climbed I heard a loud noise and looked up to see two prodigious flying beasts settling in the tree, which caused me to get down rather more hurriedly. I ask the reader not to be astonished that I call these birds "beasts"; their extraordinary size amazed me, and I am describing what I felt at the time. I flung myself headlong into the nearest bushes and cowered there, petrified by the fear of what might follow and listening to cries so piercing and terrible that I expected to be devoured at any moment. Finally, I pulled myself together and reasoned that it would be better to die quickly than to languish on in such a predicament. "After all," I said to myself, "I have to die one way or another, and I can only escape one danger by falling into another one."

So turning my eyes heavenward I said, with a heavy heart, "Lord, I thank thee for deigning to show me that thou art my Master, just as thou art my Maker. I know too, that it is proper that I make the sacrifice that thy glorification demands and that the favors I have been granted by thy Providence surpass all understanding. Truly, Lord, I cannot and ought not expect any more; indeed, the state to which I am reduced convinces me that the greatest blessing I could receive from thy paternal grace is to die without delay. Have pity, great Redeemer, on this poor creature that thou didst see fit to create and to redeem with thy precious blood and let the fate I am to meet with be the path of felicity that thou hast prepared for me."

Having finished my prayer, I got up resolved to die, and the thought that my father and mother too had died where the sea meets the land led me down to the spot where my plank lay. On leaving my refuge I was pursued by such a vast horde of creatures that I could not rightly tell what they were. However, my mind was calm and my judgment as clear as it could be under such circumstances. There seemed to be a species of horse, but with a pointed head and clawed hooves; I am not sure whether it was these same creatures that had landed in the tree above me. I believe they were feathered and had wings. In addition I could distinguish a certain kind of giant dog and several other creatures that have no like at all in Europe—all, it seemed to me, of a gay disposition and curious to see this novelty that had come among them.

I shouted in Catalan, "God preserve you, my friends!" whereupon they burst into an uproar of what seemed to be joy and excitement. I added, "You are greatly obliged to me for coming so far to entertain you and be your victim." But their clamor then increased all the more, so I resolved to sell my life at a price rather than give it away like a coward. I seized my plank and brandished it at them, which they studied attentively, until two of the biggest among them moved forward. I engaged one of them and gave it such a clout that they were obliged to retreat, and then their joyful voices turned into rude shouts.[3]

Following their withdrawal, my blood ran cold as I again heard the frightful shrieks I had heard earlier. I hastily picked three fruits from the tree I mentioned and plunged into the sea with my plank. After swimming far enough (as I thought) to be out of danger, I stopped and gazed back at the island. I saw the hoard of beasts reappear on the shore and some of them come swimming after me so fast that it seemed they must soon reach me. They fanned out into a great inverted *U,* and because I was inevitably going to be trapped, I turned on them with the end of my plank, to considerable effect. In trying to bite off the end of it, they pushed me along with them, and this continued until I was backed onto a sort of floating island, which immediately bore me out of reach of my enemies.

3. Foigny clearly parodies early scenes of culture contact, as reported in the sources he probably used.

Nonetheless, they followed with mounting courage, or rather rage, at seeing me slip out of their grasp. Finally my island ceased to move, and they were able to catch up. I had no idea where I was nor what was carrying me; but suddenly four of the great flying beasts, coming to the aid of the others in the water, descended on me. I shielded myself from their first attack with my plank, which, however, their beaks easily pierced. At that moment my island started up with such a jerk that it threw me into the sea about fifty paces away. I think it must have been a species of whale unknown to the naturalists and that one of these bird-monsters had stuck its claws into its back, causing it to leap (as I reckoned) one hundred cubits out of the water and emit a noise more terrible than thunder.[4]

This upheaval left me back in the water, and the confusion into which it threw my mind makes it difficult to say accurately what happened next. All I know is that my hooked fingers ensured that I did not let go of my plank. Coming to my senses somewhat, I again saw the beast, hissing and blowing water from what I counted to be more than one hundred paws and heads, and resembling somewhat our giant Portuguese spiders. Finally, this fish disappeared back into the sea and the birds pursuing me withdrew, so that after all these catastrophes I was left alone in the middle of the ocean, with nothing in sight to the four points of the compass under a blazing sun that was the only witness to this tragedy.[5]

---

4. One cubit was 18 inches (45 centimeters). Whales featured in tales of earlier fantastic voyages, such as Lucian's *True Story,* and in that of St. Brendan's Atlantic crossing—both are likely models for this episode.

5. The "tragedy" is, as mentioned, a symbolic birth or rebirth (in Lucian, for example, the traveler is eaten by the whale, then escapes from it to a "milk island" in a sea of milk). But Sadeur is about to reenter, in terms of this metaphor, the womb. This is what the Southern Land, with its pre-Adamic hermaphrodism—innocent of any differentiation—will signify. Note that when (p. 6) Sadeur mentions having written part of his memoirs *"right*

Any other witness would have seen a poor man exposed to the mercy of the waves, with no other resource than a piece of wood and no other thought than for his imminent death—a languishing body raw with exhaustion and swallowing so much seawater that it could not possibly survive. An observer would have seen, in fact, a man calmly resigned in his mind to the will of God; for although all these evils had befallen me and my doom seemed inevitable, I still had hope and a firm conviction that I could not die, even here in "death's dark vale."[6] I remembered my three fruits and enthusiastically ate two of them, then fell into a deep sleep, lying face up on my plank to keep from drowning.

I was in this state as I closed my eyes and have no idea how long I remained so. At length I was awakened, as I think, by the strong sunlight on my face and found myself being borne rapidly along by a northwest wind, which, although strong, did not greatly disturb the sea. I woke up with my heart so gay and my mind so relaxed that I could not help intoning the psalm "The Lord is my Light and my Salvation,"[7] which brought me such inner peace that my tears of joy mingled with the sea. I considered myself fortunate to be in God's hands and to have no other concern than his Providence.

I spent about three hours in this meditation, which was more rewarding than anything I had known, at the end of which time I made a landfall, the wind carrying me right ashore without mishap. My crooked fingers were so tightly fastened onto my plank that I could scarcely free them to climb ashore. My clothes were so sodden with seawater that I could barely wear them. The

---

in the Southern Land," the French is *à Crin*—perhaps a pun meaning both "absolutely" and the name of a place, Crin, which in terms of the Australians' language (see chap. 9) would mean "black, wet, hot, and watery" (Benrekassa 1985, 164)—that is, womb-like.

6. *Dans cet amas de morts qui m'environnoient.*

7. *"Dominus illuminatio mea et salus mea."*

time I had spent being tossed about had affected me with such a vertigo that I could barely stand up. I was like a man whom too much drinking and dancing had made giddy and incapable of putting one foot in front of the other. All I could do was drag myself four paces from the sea and lie down, awaiting whatever God had in store for his poor creature.

I passed out immediately, and a sleep (which, as far as I can judge, lasted about sixteen hours) restored my senses somewhat. I then remembered that I still had one of my fruits left and, having eaten it, realized that my weakened state was largely due to starvation. I therefore set off into the island to look for something, and after only about two hundred paces found several trees which, however, had no fruit—either because they were actually fruitless or because my eyes were so weakened that they could no longer discern fruit. I prostrated myself on the ground and mumbled desperately, "Lord, hast thou preserved me through so many perils on the sea and brought me to land only to let me starve here? Well, thy will be done; I will gladly die, so long as it be thy will." I had just finished this prayer and was looking around for a spot to lie down and await the end of my wretched life, when I spied two fruits covered with leaves. I took them as a gift from Heaven and a sure sign that God did not wish me to perish yet.

Having eaten one, I gained the strength to carry on and to estimate my whereabouts, which I judged to be around the 35th austral parallel. I noticed several indications that the southern continent was not far away—the seawater was fairly fresh;[8] the winds were blowing from the south and came in irregular gusts bringing certain extraordinary fragrances—in a word, I was

---

8. One of the signs that indicated to navigators the proximity of a large river, such as the Amazon. Fresh-water ocean, as a metaphor signifying purity, features in a Hellenistic work by Iambulus that was among Foigny's sources.

confident of having found land. Advancing farther, I found a tree so laden with plump fruit that its branches were bowed to the ground, and the place was carpeted with a kaleidoscope of fragrant flowers. As soon as I had eaten these fruits, I fainted and fell asleep, or rather was hypnotized in such a way that I perceived and understood everything going on around me without being either touched or moved by it.

Presently I heard a chorus of voices, which aroused in me an indescribable sensation. Then I saw seven beasts the size and color of bears, except that each of their paws was as big as their head. They seemed to approach me and then, without touching me, to withdraw; this was repeated several times. Finally, they set about devouring me in earnest, and I was already covered in blood when two of the giant birds I described previously came down and caused these creatures to take refuge in some holes nearby. The birds spent some time trying to get them out, but then, thwarted in their efforts, turned on me. After dealing me a few blows, one of them sank its claws into me and hoisted me into the air. Fortunately, the several layers of leather girdle I was wearing around my midriff protected me from being pierced through to my entrails. I had by now fully regained my normal state through enduring these indescribable trials.

After a long flight these creatures alighted on a rock where the one carrying me let go to pass the burden to its companion. The pain of the similar treatment I received from the latter became unbearable, and in a fit of fury I went for its throat and then was able to tear out its eyes with my teeth. Blinded, it fell into the water and made no further attempt to pick me up, so I climbed onto its back. Its companion had gone on ahead, but on noticing that we were not following but rather sitting in the water, it turned back and fell on me with unbelievable ferocity. It perched on my shoulders and delivered blows that would have been fatal had they found their mark. I had in by girdle a small dagger, which I was able to thrust into its belly by finding a

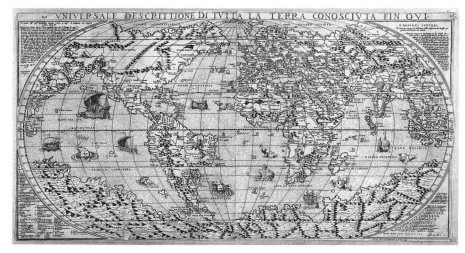

1. Forlani-Duchetti, *Universale descrittione . . .* (1570),
a typical southern-continent fantasy. Another version of it shows
real and imaginary animals in the continent.
Courtesy of the Newberry Library.

vulnerable spot (for a remarkable fact about these birds is that
they are almost impenetrable on account of the split shell that
encloses and protects them as we shall see presently).

While I was dealing with this second adversary, the first slid
from between my thighs and took off, but I clung to one of its legs
and, although raised high into the air, hung on for dear life. It
screeched horribly, like a beast being killed, and after soaring
high plunged down again into the sea. There I had a chance to go
for its throat and then get onto its back again. It bellowed as it
bled and belabored me as skillfully as might a man of great
judgment, trying to either drown me or throw me off. It twisted,
leaped, and somersaulted in its efforts to get rid of me. My only
thought was to hang on like grim death because my plank was
gone and without that support and safeguard I would surely
drown. Finally, the beast grew still, confessing its defeat. I then

had a chance to survey my wounds and found that there was not a single part of my body without bloody lacerations. My clothes were torn to shreds; I was left naked. The seawater, even though fairly fresh in these parts, was yet salty enough to sting in my wounds, and I passed out from the pain.

I found out later that some of the Australian coast guard had watched part of this combat, and four of them had been sent in a boat to investigate. Thinking I was dead, they pulled me aboard; but as soon as they realized that I was still alive, they introduced a certain fluid into my mouth, nose, ears, and fundament, which immediately opened my eyes and revealed my benefactors to me. Then they gave me a drink that, even as I drank it, restored my vigor. They washed my body with scented water and dressed and bandaged my wounds. Having got me out of danger, they chased my enemies, dragging the second of them into the boat and laying it at my feet. The other one was still alive and, when I told them by sign-language that I had torn out its eyes, they got it aboard as well and laid the two together with seemingly inexplicable conjoinment.[9] Then they returned to the shore, which was about three hours away. On our arrival they made a formal presentation of me, with the dead birds at my feet, calling the episode in their language the "Miraculous Victory of the Conqueror."

---

9. *Conjoflissance:* a neologism combining elements such as *jouissance* (pleasure) or *jolifier* (to enliven). It was commuted in the 1692 version to *réjouissance* (enjoyment). Ronzeaud (1990, 62) notes that *conjouir* was in dictionaries of the period, with the sense of a joyful welcome.

CHAPTER FOUR

A Description of the Southern Land

$\mathbb{I}$f anything should cause us to admire divine Providence, it is the story I have just related where everything seemed to conspire to lead me to the Southern Land. Thus, a series of shipwrecks was necessary to train me to endure them; my hermaphrodism would ensure my survival when I arrived there, as we shall see, and my nakedness too would prevent me from being recognized as an alien and killed. Again, without the glory I had acquired in their eyes through my battle with the birds, I would have had to undergo a very rigorous examination leading, without doubt, to my execution. All in all, one would have to admit, taking into account all the circumstances and perils of my voyage, the working in them of God's will, which infallibly disposes his creatures toward the ends it proposes, even when it appears otherwise.[1]

The custom of these people is to receive among themselves only those whose birthplace, nation, and ways are known to

---

1. The theological tone seems excessive by modern standards and may have been parodic. Whatever the case, the effect is lost in the 1692 text in which, for example, "the ways of God" is replaced with "a certain order of things in the destiny of men and a chaining together of effects so that nothing can prevent its succession."

them, but their admiration for my valiant struggle meant that I was admitted without question into the nearest community where everyone came to kiss my hands and "parts." They wanted to carry me above their heads in a triumphal procession in accordance with their custom but refrained when they realized how much discomfort that would cause me. After my reception, those that had rescued and cared for me took me to their Heb, which could be translated "House of Education." There my board and lodging were provided for with a thoroughness and decency surpassing any in Europe.

Scarcely had I arrived when two hundred young Australians came to greet me in a gay and engaging manner. As I was recovering from my ordeal, I was eager to communicate and utter some words I remembered from the Congo: *rim lem,* meaning "I am your servant." This, however, was interpreted by them as an oracular revelation that I was "from the land above."[2] Accordingly, they joyfully shouted, "The key! The key!" (Our brother! Our brother!).[3] I was given two fruits of scarlet red tinted with blue, and upon eating one I felt agreeably fortified. Then they gave me a sort of yellowish drinking pouch, holding about one glassful of a beverage that I drank with a pleasure I had never before known.

Among these new faces in this new land, I was like a man fallen from the sky,[4] and I could scarcely believe that what I was seeing was real. Sometimes I said to myself that I must be either dead or mad, and even when I managed to convince myself that I was indeed alive and sane, I could not believe that I was in a land and among people of the same nature as in Europe. After a fortnight I was fully recovered, and in five months I had learned

2. *Je suis du pays supérieur.* This mention of a "land above" (Heaven? Europe?) was omitted in the 1692 version.

3. *Le clé (la clé* is a feminine noun in French).

4. *tombé des nuës.*

enough of the language to be able to communicate with them. Here then are the geographical details of the Southern Land as I understood them from my sources there and can describe them in terms of Ptolemy's system.[5]

Commencing around the 340th meridian at 52 degrees south latitude, it rises toward the equator through forty meridians to reach 40 degrees south; all this part is called Huff. The coast continues at this latitude for about fifteen degrees of longitude, this part being named Hubc. From there the sea advances again through a further twenty-five meridians down to 51 degrees south, and this entire west-facing coast is known as Hump. The sea then forms a large gulf called Slab, after which the land rises again over four meridians, to forty-two and one-half degrees, forming an easterly coast, Hued. The land maintains this latitude for a further thirty-six meridians, forming a region called Huod. After this long stretch the sea gains the upper hand again, and within three meridians the coast falls away to 49 degrees south, forming a semicircular gulf extending over five meridians, and then a further six meridians bring the land back up to 30 degrees south. The west-facing part of these coasts is called Hug, the bottom of the gulf, Pug, and the other coast, Pur. After this the land continues for about thirty-four meridians at almost the same latitude with the name Sub. Then the sea seems to gather strength as, more powerful than usual, it invades the land completely and thrusts down almost to the pole, the land giving way progressively until the 160th meridian. On this coast are found the regions of Sug, Pulg, and Mulg. Around the 54th parallel is situated the mouth of the river Sulm, which forms a considerable gulf. On the banks of this river live a people quite similar to Europeans, ruled by several kings.

---

5. A second-century A.D. Alexandrian geographer who compiled the first atlas based on a grid system.

That is what I have been able to learn of some of the northern coasts of the continent. As for the polar end of the country, this contains prodigious mountains far higher and more inaccessible than the Pyrenees between France and Spain. They are called the Juads, and rise from around the 50th parallel or, sixty-five meridians away, from the 60th, or, farther on again, from 48 degrees and 50 degrees south. Their northern limit then extends to 48 degrees south before falling back to 55 degrees, after which they reach as far north as 43 degrees before ending in the sea. At the foot of these mountains can be found the following regions: Curf, extending from the mountains as far as Huff; followed by Gurf, Durf, Iurf, and Sur, which extends right to the coast. In the middle part of the country between the mountains and the coast are found Hum, Sum, Burd, Purd, Rurf, Furf, Iurf,[6] and Pulg, which ends at the coast. Altogether there are twenty-seven large regions, totaling about three thousand leagues in length and four to five thousand in breadth.

The valley that lies beyond these mountains is between ten and twenty degrees wide and divided by two rivers with large estuaries: one flowing westwards, called Sulms, the other eastward, called Sulm.[7] The length of this region is about eight hundred leagues, its width up to six hundred but, on average, three hundred. All of this vast land is called Fund and is ruled by ten or twelve kings, who regularly engage in cruel wars against each other and seek to invade the other austral lands.[8]

6. Or "Jurf"; *I* and *J* were interchangeable in early scripts. The 1692 edition omits this name from the list, presumably because it duplicates that in the previous sentence.

7. The 1692 edition has "Sulm" for the former and "Hulm" for the latter.

8. Compare to Plato's Atlantis, comprising ten provinces ruled by kings descended from the sea god Poseidon, or to a more specifically antipodean utopia of the period by Theopompus (see Fausett 1993, chap. 2).

Most remarkable of all is that the interior of the Southern Land is without a single mountain, and I was told that the Australians had flattened them all. To this miracle of artifice or nature must be added their admirable uniformity of language, custom, architecture, and agriculture throughout this vast land. To know one region is to know them all, and this arises from the natural inclination of the inhabitants to seek nothing more than their fellows so that even if one of them had something out of the ordinary, it would be impossible for him to use it.[9]

Altogether there are fifteen thousand *seizains*[10] in this immense land. Each contains sixteen quarters, not counting the Hab[11] and the four Hebs, or "Houses of Education." There are twenty-five houses in each quarter, each containing four divisions that each accommodates four individuals.[12] Thus there are four hundred houses in each seizain with sixty-four hundred persons, which, multiplied by the fifteen thousand seizains, gives a total of ninety-six million. To this must be added the young people living with their masters in the Hebs, about eight hundred in each, so that in the sixty thousand Hebs live a further forty-eight million, consisting of pupils and masters.

The central edifice of the seizain, the Hab, or "House of Elevation," is built entirely of a transparent stone that could be compared to our finest rock crystal except that it is shot through with unimaginable streaks of green and gold to form images of people, landscapes, heavenly bodies, and other figures so realisitic

9. The latter detail was emphasized in missionary primitivism of the time (see chap. 5, n. 1). Artificial landscapes were a central theme in More's *Utopia* (see Marin [1984, 99–111]).

10. Literally, "sixteens."

11. Pronounced "hub" in French; and the temple is indeed the hub, both spatial and ideological, of the community. This may not be coincidental, given that Foigny was a linguist.

12. On Foigny's complex use of numerology, see Ronzeaud 1982a, 262–70, 292, 301ff.

that I would not be believed even if I were able to describe them. The entire building is without any other artifice than the highly polished finish of this stone. It has seating all around its interior with sixteen large tables of a red that surpasses our purple in richness.[13] It has four main entrances corresponding to the four great roads that intersect at it. The beauty of its exterior is as subtle as it is fine, consisting of one thousand stepped terraces that can be climbed, leading to a summit that is a sort of platform able to accommodate forty people. The paving of this superb edifice is not unlike our jasper although brighter in color and with veins of a rich blue and a yellow brighter than gold. Nobody lives there, but the quarters take daily turns in setting a table for twelve persons so that visitors might be readily received. It is situated in the center of the seizain and is about 100 paces in diameter or 313 around.

The communal building shared by four quarters called the Heb, or House of Education, is entirely built of the material that forms the floor of the Hab except for its roof, which is of a transparent stone that lets in light and illumination. Its flooring is somewhat like our white marble but with flecks of red and green. This handsome building is divided into four equal segments by two internal walls and is situated at the junction of the four quarters. It is fifty paces in diameter and about fifty-three around,[14] a pace being five and one-half feet and each foot containing thirteen royal toes, or inches. Each segment is for the youth of the quarter it faces, and in it at least two hundred youngsters are carefully raised together. The

13. Red commonly signified the sacred in tribal society, whereas purple was the color of royalty in Europe. This section also had a biblical basis (see introduction, n. 40).

14. An apparently deliberate illogicality, like others to come, this was reproduced in 1692 (despite other modifications to, and omissions from, these descriptions). Ronzeaud (loc. cit.) attempts to find a rational explanation, but it is unlikely that Foigny intended one (cf. introduction, n. 44).

"mothers" accompany their "fruits" until two years after their conception.

The youngsters are divided into five bands or age sets: the first mastering the first principles under the tutorship of six masters; the second studying the logic appropriate to things natural under four masters; the third comprising those permitted to reason, who have two masters; the fourth, those who have mastered dialectic,[15] having only one master; and the fifth group, those waiting to become "lieutenants," that is, to take the place of a brother retiring from this world, as I shall explain.

The people's food is provided by the members of each quarter, who regularly bring in to their morning assembly whatever is needed by their numerous family.

The communal dwelling houses that they call Hiebs, or "men's houses," number twenty-five in each quarter; each is twenty-five paces in diameter and about eighty around. They are divided, like the Hebs, by two main walls forming four identical segments, each ending in an apartment.[16] Their construction is entirely of the white marble that forms the floor of the Heb except for the windows, which are of the clear crystal of the Hab to let in light. Each segment is inhabited by four persons who call each other *key* (brother). There is nothing inside these spaces except the four benches they sleep on and seven or eight chairs.

The garden areas that they call Huids are about three hundred paces around the sixty-five across. In form they are perfectly square and divided by twelve handsome boulevards enclosing progressively smaller areas down to a central square six paces across. The first three of these, the longest, are planted with trees at intervals of five feet bearing fruits considered to be the least valuable. These are as big as our Portuguese calabashes, seven to eight inches in diameter. Their flesh is red and tastier than our greatest delicacies with a juice like the sweetest orange

---

15. *Ceux qui peuvent opposer* (1692, *composer*).
16. *Département* (1692, *appartement*).

juice, and one of these fruits is ample to feed four men, however hungry. The next five rows are planted with bushes that produce the small yellowish drinking vessels filled with a remarkably refreshing and fortifying liquor. One of these suffices to quench the thirst, but three are usually drunk at each meal. The last four rows are filled with small bushes bearing a berrylike fruit of an unheard-of fragrance, taste, and purple color. It has the property of inducing[17] sleep according to the number eaten so that they are in the habit of taking one in the evening and being induced to sleep for three hours.

Along each thoroughfare they dig two shallow trenches in which they grow root crops, producing fruits of three sorts: some resembling our finest melons, others fat like bon chretien pears but marvelously blue, and the third like our little Spanish courgettes although of entirely different color and taste.

Such is the produce that sustains the inhabitants of every part of that vast land. They know neither oven nor pot nor what it means to cook food. Their fruits satisfy their needs and tastes completely, without causing any indigestion or offense to their stomachs because they eat them perfectly ripe[18] and with no trace of tartness.[19]

One tree growing in the central square stands out from the rest, both in height and because of its remarkable fruit. These, the size of olives and reddish, are called Balf, or "Tree of Joy." If four of them are eaten, one becomes intoxicated, whereas six induce a sleep lasting twenty-four hours. If one exceeds this dose, the sleep becomes eternal. But it is preceded by such an ecstasy of drunken joy that, to see them in this state, you would think that for them death was the greatest boon in the world. They rarely sing during their lives and never dance, but this fruit makes them sing and dance all the way to the grave.

17. *D'exciter* (1692, *causer*).
18. *Cuits* (cooked) (1692, *meurs* [ripe]).
19. *Verdure* (1692, *verdeur*).

I should mention that all of these trees bear ripe fruit at all times, being laden with ripe and ripening fruit and with flowers and buds. We know something of the sort with our orange-trees, except that the rigors of our winters and the ardors of our summers affect them considerably, whereas in this land it is difficult to perceive any seasonal variation.

From these facts, indeed, it is easy to deduce that the country is entirely flat, without forests, swamps, or deserts, and evenly populated throughout. Nor will it come as a surprise that it slopes evenly down from the pole to the sea with a gradient of only about three in four or five thousand leagues. This slope continues on into the sea, moreover, which is so shallow for a distance of three leagues or so from the shore that it can barely admit any vessel. At the coast it is only one finger's depth, and after a league it has increased to one foot, and so on. Hence, apart from a few channels known only to the locals, this land is impossible to approach from the sea.[20]

The same gradient means that the whole of this prodigious country lies to the sun, which provides an energy matching the even fertility of the soil everywhere. It can easily be seen, too, that the mountains rising toward the pole were sculpted from nature for the express purpose of sheltering and irrigating the land. Furthermore, these forbidding ramparts serve to capture the sun's rays and reflect them onto the most polar parts. In this way is achieved that incomparably good fortune, of which northerns are deprived, of having no excesses of cold in winter nor of heat in summer, in other words, of not having seasons.

I have no doubt that this proposition will surprise the geographers, who, having divided the earth into two equal halves

20. These topographical indications correspond to what seems to have been known of Australia at the time: its west coast reefs, which had claimed a number of ships; its flat and barren interior; and its northeastern *coste dangereuse* (as the famous Dieppe maps named it, perhaps referring to the Great Barrier Reef).

2. A distinguished predecessor—Joseph Hall's Viraginia,
a province of his imaginary southern continent with its
Island of Hermaphrodites, in *Mundus alter et idem* (1605).
Courtesy of the Newberry Library

by means of the line they call the equinoctial, assume as much
heat and cold in one hemisphere as in the other on the basis that
winter and summer consist of the distance or proximity of the
sun. Some, however, have corrected this error: even without
knowing of the Southern Land, they have pointed out that if this
were so, then Guinea, Abyssinia, and the Moluccas would at all
times receive more heat than Portugal and Italy because the sun
is never far distant, whereas travelers and cosmologists alike
assert that the hot season is more properly the time of the dog
days[21] and that excessive cold is more usual under the signs of
Aquarius and Pisces than under Capricorn,[22] even though the sun
at the latter time is farther away.

21. July–August, the time of the ascendancy of the constellation Sirius.
22. That is, in January–February, rather than December.

It has to be admitted, then, that summer and winter are both constantly present but differently realized according to local conditions and that the sun has relatively little effect on the seasons because when it is closest, its heat is relatively less intense than when it is farther away. We know that in Europe the heat of May and June is less than that of July and August when the sun is past its highest elevation. There has to be another reason explaining the heat we associate with it because we can sometimes freeze in bright sunshine or be hot at night when there is no sun. When the sun heats, it is because of the other influences that accompany it.

From this principle follows the explanation of the Australian case. Whereas the summer sun in Europe burns because of the burning stars that accompany it, it is at the same time weakened in its effect on the Southern Land by being farther away in the northern hemisphere. And when it moves to the southern hemisphere, it is no longer accompanied by the burning stars so that its heat is mitigated in Australia while Europe freezes. This gives rise to a sort of perpetual summer in that rich land, bringing everything to perfection at all times (although in truth one does notice that the air is drier around July–August and cooler in January–February when ripening slows down slightly).[23]

Rain is unknown in these parts, as in Africa; there is no thunder, and scarcely a cloud is ever seen. There are no flies, caterpillars, or any kind of insect, and they do not know spiders, snakes, or other venomous creatures. In a word, it is an earthly paradise that, while containing all the riches and curiosities imaginable, is exempt from the irritations of our world.

23. This baroque cosmology (effectively omitted in 1692) is traced by Ronzeaud (1990, 79) to Renty (1657), who linked the sun's movements to those of the zodiac, around a fixed earth.

CHAPTER FIVE

The Australians and Their Customs

Each Australian has both sexes, and if a child happens to be born with only one, they kill it as a monster. Their bodies are firm, nimble, and very active, of a color closer to red than to vermilion. They average about eight feet in height. Their faces are moderately long with a broad forehead and bug eyes, a small mouth with lips redder than coral, and a nose more full than long. Their hair and beards are always black, and never cut because they grow little. Their chins are double and crooked, their necks slender, their shoulders high and muscular. Their nipples are rounded and prominent and vermilion rather than red. Their arms are sinewy; their hands broad, long, and six-fingered; their chests high; their stomachs flat and little distended by pregnancy. Their hips are high and their thighs thick, and their long legs end in six-toed feet. In some areas they are found with an extra pair of arms coming out of their hips, thinner but just as long as the other pair; these they can extend at will and thereby grip more tightly than the others.

Their total nudity comes so naturally to them that even the suggestion of covering the body is considered hostile to nature and an insult to reason.

They are obliged to present at least one child to the Heb, but they produce them in a manner so secret that it is a crime among them to speak of "conjunction" with each other to that end, and I have never been able to work out how they manage to procreate. They all love each other eagerly and in equal measure, and I can vouch that in the thirty years that I have been among them, I have witnessed neither quarrel nor difference of any sort. They do not know the meaning of *thine* and *mine*,[1] all is held in common with such complete sincerity that it surpasses even the intimacy of man and woman among Europeans.

I have always felt free to speak my mind but was too forward in expressing my astonishment to various brothers and in putting forward reasons to support my views. I spoke of their nudity with a certain disapproval, and desired to arouse them to what we call pleasure. I asked fairly pointedly where the fathers of their children were and let my displeasure be known at their silence on this matter. These and other instances were enough to turn the Australians against me, and some openly declared that I was a half-man and should be done away with.

This would indeed have happened but for the intervention of a venerable old man named Suains, the master of the third order[2] in my Heb. I know that this worthy man defended my cause several times in the assemblies of the Hab, having witnessed my combat with the birds. Seeing that I persisted in scandalizing the brothers, he took me aside one day and said in a grave voice, "We no longer have any doubt that you are one of the monsters; your wicked ways

1. This principle, insisted on by early primitivists such as Las Casas, Montaigne, or missionaries, greatly influenced seventeenth-century and Enlightenment social thought. Its first modern formulation was by Peter Martyr, whose *De Orbe Novo* appeared soon after Columbus reported his encounters with the American Indians (see Cro 1990). Again, a parody of real culture is evident here.

2. That is, of those "allowed to reason," not those "who had mastered dialectic."

and rude words have made you hated among us. We have never known such a criminal as you. For a long time now there has been talk of destroying you and were it not for your actions before our eyes, you would have been done away with straightaway on arrival here. Tell me frankly, if you can, who you are and how you came to be here." The foreboding I felt at hearing this, along with my obligation to him, caused me to make clean breast of my whole story and the adventures that had brought me to those parts.

The old man then took pity on me and assured me that if I would be more restrained in my actions and speech, the past would be forgotten; adding that he would stay alive two years longer to protect me, and that as his lieutenant was still young he would nominate me in his place. "I know," he said, "that you were astounded to arrive in a land where the customs are so different from yours, and because it is an inviolable law among us to tolerate no half-men, it is only your having both sexes that has saved you. And yet you stand condemned by your behavior, which you must correct if you wish to stay alive. I suggest, as an expedient, that you come to me as your confessor and discuss your problems, which I shall answer as best I can provided that you promise to be discrete and not provoke the brothers' anger any more." I promised my utmost fidelity and devotion, and that I would be careful not to shock anyone. This he accepted, saying that he would be my mother[3] for as long as he could protect me.

"To set a tone of candor in our discussions," he said, "let me tell you that having watched your combat, I was convinced that you were not a half-man: firstly, because I could see that you were brave; secondly, because I saw you without the coverings they wear; thirdly, I saw that you had all the marks of a whole man; fourthly, you had a wide forehead and a face like ours; and fifthly, I have noticed ever since that you think about things. These qualities have preserved you since the time you were found to be

---

3. 1692: "father."

malicious. So tell me: firstly, how you live in your country; secondly, if everyone there is like you in body and mind; thirdly, if the clothing fetish we have noticed among foreigners is outlawed; fourthly, if avarice and ambition are proscribed. Fifthly, explain the customs and ways of your country to me without disguising them in any way, as you promised."

I was convinced that, under the circumstances, to deceive him would put both his life and mine in danger. So I thought it best to answer simply and without giving him any cause for suspicion. I outlined the geography of my country, of the great continent we inhabit with its names of Asia, Europe, and Africa. Then I went on at length about the multitude of animal species, among which the old man admired most the ones we despise— gnats, lice, fleas, and so forth—filled with wonder that such tiny creatures could enjoy independent life and movement. I described the various foods we eat, from which he drew the conclusion familiar to our doctors: that we could not live long because our systems are kept to no dietary régime, leaving our blood weak and our bodies exposed to illnesses and early death. This I granted him, adding that it was rare for any northerner to reach eighty but that nature made up for this by an abundance of procreation, a single individual often producing up to ten or twelve children.

He passed over this matter, anxious to move on to others. I told him that hermaphrodism was so rare among us that it was considered monstrous. As for reasoning, I said that it was cultivated by some individuals and that public lessons on it were given in various places. Here he interrupted, saying, "You go either too fast or too slow; be careful not to get bogged down in contradictions. You cannot reconcile the exercise of reason with the exclusion of one of the genders,[4] and when you add that some

4. On the relationship between the "neuter" or "neutral" (both trans- lated *neutre* in French) and rationality, particularly as theorized later by Kant, see Marin (1984, 14–26).

among you reason and that reasoning is taught in some places, you merely prove that reason is entirely absent among you. The first fruit of reason is to know oneself, and this knowledge necessarily includes two things: firstly, that to be a man one must be whole; and secondly, that one must be free to reason when and where one wants. You fall short of the first because all your people are imperfect and of the second because you have only a few who can reason. Can you deny these objections?"

I replied that it was a principle of reasoning to call a thing perfect that had everything its essence required[5] and that to try to include everything that can be imagined was to produce only a monstrous effect. "For example," I said, "you would not say that a man lacks perfection because he is not the sun; this would be to introduce confusion into nature so that nothing could then be perfect. It is, therefore, necessary to know what the criteria of human perfection are to make judgments as to the defective and the perfect."

"You speak well," he replied, "and you seem to realize that man is two things: a body more perfect than that of any animal and a mind more enlightened. Bodily perfection means all that the body can and must be, without deformity, whereas that of the mind extends man's knowledge over all that there is to be known or at least provides the reasoning faculty by which such extension can be achieved. But will you not grant that it is a greater perfection to hold together all that is needed for man's perfection rather than divide it? To make a whole man requires both sexes; why then do you represent to me as two men what is in fact only one? Can we not rightly say that those two are imperfect because they only represent a half?"

I replied that we should consider man as one of the animals, as far as his body was concerned, and that, just as an animal cannot rightly be called imperfect for having only one sex, so it cannot reasonably be said that man is imperfect in not having both sexes.

---

5. *Tout ce qui étoit requis à son établissement.*

On the contrary, the confusion of the two sexes in a single individual could only be considered defective and monstrous rather than a mark of perfection.

"Your reasoning," he replied, "proves that you are the beasts we think you are although you yourself cannot reasonably be called such because you show some signs of humanity. The most that can be said, without sparing the truth, is that you are half-men. Your proposition that we are like the animals in body is an error, and to separate man's mind and body as if they were two discrete entities is an even greater error. The union of these two parts is such that each is absorbed into the other, and just as no operation imaginable could ever extract from man's body a part that was not human and did not distinguish him from the animals, so you would have to agree that man is distinguished from beast by all that is specifically human and that he has no quality that is not his alone to the exclusion of all animals."

He saw that I was unwilling to pursue the matter further, but when he signaled that I should be satisfied with that, I added, "Can you deny that man partakes of animality in his flesh, bone and senses? That both have flesh, vision, and hearing and that we indeed experience them every time we think about it?"

"Yes," he replied, "we formally deny it; man has no human quality that could be shared by the animals. All your chimerical conceptions are only weaknesses of your reasoning, which brings together what cannot be joined and often separates what is inseparable. For example, when you state that flesh in general applies equally to man and to animal, you would have us understand that the word flesh can be applied to both on account of some quality common to both. But only a weak mind would make such an analogy, which is a manifest contradiction because it is impossible for one thing to be another, however they be understood. So you must admit that the animal is animal and resembles other animals, most particularly in the fact that their sexes are separate and must reunite to procreate. This division of essences can be overcome by a perfect union only if the latter can be a single identity; otherwise, the product of such union must itself be imperfect because the natural need for the two sexes to come together causes them to seek each other and to languish in the other's absence. As for us, we are completely whole, and there is none among us who does not have all of the human parts fully formed, which means that we live without those animal passions and cannot even stand hearing about them. This means that we can live alone contentedly, having no need of one another, and that our relations with each other are never carnal."

I could not hear the man's words without remembering what our theology teaches about the production of the second person of the Trinity, and all its effects outside of divinity. I went over and over these great principles of our philosophy: that the more perfect a being, the less it needs to act, and the more it imitates in this its Creator, which acts only through its productions. That the concourse[6] of two beings to procreate a single one cannot be without serious problems because the uniting of two active principles to produce a single effect necessarily means a hierarchy of active and passive: a combat, a play of refusal and coupling that can only end up passing on the same weaknesses and conflict to the product of the union.

He could see from my abstracted look that I was beginning to absorb his reasoning. So changing, or rather abandoning, that tack, he asked, "Supposing that two beings did collaborate to produce a child, to which would it rightfully belong?" I replied that it belonged to them both by an indivisible right, and gave the example of many animal species that show by their joint caring that their offspring belong to them both. But he indignantly rejected this example and forbade me to use it any more on pain of ending the discussion, because it confirmed just what he was saying, namely, that our kind are more beast than man and could at the

6. *Concurrence.*

most be regarded as half-men. He added that this natural marriage must endure great difficulties because the two wills could not easily be reconciled and many disputes would arise.

I replied that there was indeed much subordination in the relationship, the mother and child being subject to the father. But because the word *father* is unknown to the Australians and I had to more or less forge an expression that would convey my meaning, he made me repeat it three times over and, for fear of misunderstanding, explained to me what he had understood by it. After which he was utterly convinced of the common Australian view that we could not be human, shouting with extraordinary severity, "Hey, where is your judgment? Where is reason? Where is the human? Where is the human?" repeated three times over. I said that the laws of the land had ordained it thus—not without a certain justification, in that the primary cause should be put first, the father being the primary principle of generation.[7]

"Let us examine that proposition rigorously," he said. "You said that the two acted together to procreate, and you gave me to understand that the action took place inside the mother. How then can you assert that the father acts before the mother? If they act together, where is the primacy? If there is primacy, on what grounds can it be attributed to the father? If everything happens within the mother, why not consider her the first principle? Would it not be more logical to regard the supposed father as a secondary cause[8] and the mother, in whom everything takes place and without whom all would be impossible, as the true cause? And tell me, is the mother so attached to this father that she cannot receive another?" I replied candidly that this was indeed a road upon which many traveled with as much liberty as the mother was prepared to give.

7. A common biological assumption at the time was that the female functioned only as a receptacle in procreation.

8. *Condition étrangère.*

"That is another reason for the extreme absurdity that you all fall into," he went on. "On what basis can this supposed first principle lay claim to being as you describe it? He has to have recourse to a second principle, and in this way the second becomes the first; nor could you grant him this priority, it seems, without doing an injustice to four or five others."

I can assure the reader that I was greatly affected by the old man's arguments, and although I could not agree with them (for they overturned all our laws), they certainly set me thinking, especially about our severe treatment of the sex that nature owes so much to. My thoughts gave me plenty of reason to agree with the old philosopher, and I was forced to admit that the great empire that the male has usurped over the female was rather a form of tyranny than a just cause.

The first part of the argument being exhausted, we entered into the second, which concerned the northerners' powers of reasoning. But he spoke as if that issue too were already decided, thinking that he had convinced me on the previous point—that we could not be whole men. "What caused me to suspect that you were not has now become fully clear," he said. "However, because it cannot be denied that you have shown outstanding qualities, I need to know where they come from in your background and your reasoning." I assured him that what he had seen me do was done more out of despair than of any habitual courage, and that there were no such birds to fight in our regions. There, combat was waged between equals, and with many cruel refinements and butcheries.

"So, they are just like the Fundians,"[9] he said, and when I agreed, he added, "You have been among us now for long enough to know us and be convinced about our ways. The name *man,* with

9. Inhabitants of the region of Fund; whose name ("Fondins" in the French) seems to allude to the "fundament" or anus *(fondement).* The meaning of this interpretation will become clearer as the story progresses.

its necessary corollaries of reason and humanity, obliges us to maintain such unity among ourselves that we do not even know discord or division. Thus you would have to admit either that we are more than men or that you are less than men because you fall so far short of our perfection." I admitted that regional differences contribute greatly to the varied inclinations of our peoples, making some less bilious, others more active, some stolid, others frivolous, and so forth, this being a major cause of our disputes and wars and of all the evils they bring. But he violently rejected this excuse, saying that man, in being man, remains everywhere and at all times man, that is to say, human, reasonable, debonair, and phlegmatic. It is in this that man's nature consists. Just as the sun cannot be a sun without illuminating and water cannot be water without being wet, so man cannot be human without differing from the animals in that they are full of passions and faults from which man should be exempt. The infallible proof that a man is less than human—merely a vain and deceitful mask of humanity—is when he gets carried away in quarrels, greed, luxury, or other vices. His true essence consists in exemption from these bestial failings, and he is more or less a man inasmuch as he is more or less prone to vice.

I must confess that I could only listen with admiration to all of this, even more so than if I had been reading a very eloquent book or hearing a powerful orator. I recalled the fine passage in Ecclesiastes[10] that tells us that "the being of man consists in keeping God's covenant," without which he is no longer man but only a deceptive image of man.

When he questioned me about this, I replied that I had, in fact, been well schooled in spiritual matters and that nothing had been spared for my enlightenment. He asked whether the same

10. Eccles. 12:13. The King James version of this passage loses its original sense, of an *essence* of man *("hoc est enim omnis homo"),* by translating it "for this is the whole *duty* of man." Cf. the concluding paragraphs of the introduction.

concern was extended to everyone, and on learning that it was not, he reiterated that this inequality was the cause of the divisions that led to all our problems, disorders and disputes—because he who knows less, seeing himself placed beneath those who know more, feels all the more deprived for knowing that nature created them all equal. "As for us," he added, "we profess equality in all things; our glory lies in appearing identical and equally cultivated in all things. The only distinction we seek is in our experiments so as to discover some subtlety or secret of use to the community."

He questioned me next on my early life. I said very little about it because I had already told him that, far from giving me any particular virtue or advantage over others, it had rather been that of a weakling. Then he passed on to the matter of our "superfluities." I knew that by these he meant the clothes worn by Europeans, and I assured him that we were as horrified to see people without clothes as the Australians were to see people with them. I gave as reasons for this custom our climate and our modesty. He could readily see that custom might exert such an influence on our minds as to make us unable to change habits acquired in our youth without doing ourselves a great violence. I then reminded him that the European lands suffered extremes of cold that were unbearable to bodies more delicate than those of the Australians—that we even sometimes died of it, and that survival would be impossible without covering ourselves. Finally, I added that the moral weakness of both sexes was such that they could not see each other naked without experiencing certain emotions that decency obliges one to leave unsaid.

"There is some logic in what you say," he replied, "but where does this 'custom' come from? How has it come about that an entire world could embrace what is so contrary to nature? We are born as what we are and could only cover ourselves through believing that we are unworthy to be seen. As for accepting your argument about the rigors of the seasons, I cannot and, indeed, should not. For if the country is so unbearable, nothing obliges a rational being to make it his home, and he can only sink lower than the beasts by staying in a place that does him violence, especially when he knows that he is mortal. Nature, in making an animal, gives it freedom of movement to seek what it needs and to flee danger. So when it persists in staying in a place where it is menaced on all sides and must be continually on the defensive to survive, it cannot have any reasoning powers—at least if I have any.

"As for the weakness you speak of, there can be nothing further to say about it because you admit so ingenuously what I have been trying to convince you of by rational argument. It is only a weakness dragging you below the level of beasts, indeed, that could justify the ardors you mention. The beasts see each other too, but this sight does not affect them. How then can it be that you, who place yourselves above them, could be weaker than the weakest? Have you so little insight as not to be able to see through such coverings? Even a brute has more feelings than that; a mere veil will never prevent it from pursuing its desires.

"Judging your people by the little you have told me, they have a slight tincture of reason but not enough to be enlightened by it. If it be true that they cannot inhabit their lands without wearing furs, then they behave like those who, to avoid fleeing an obvious danger, rationalize their way into a thousand and one excuses. If it be true that clothes can keep them wise and chaste, they imitate small children who are no longer aware of an object once it is hidden. But reason always finds its way and penetrates to the bottom of things; no such obstacle can hold it back, and it resigns itself to circumstances only when forced to.[11] If its dwelling place is threatened, it does not seek palliatives, but the means of fleeing. And if it is determined in its pursuit of an object, no shadow or veil will obstruct it. The most beautiful

----

11. *Le raisonnement ne s'attache à la circonstance que lors qu'il ne peut éviter le principal.*

thing in man's eyes is man himself, and it is only the beauty of his "parts" that makes him so. As soon as they are covered, they are declared unworthy to be seen. In a word, I could never be made to believe that what is held to be an object of desire could rightfully be hidden."

I listened to the man rather as to an oracle than to a philosopher; all his propositions appeared to be based on invincible arguments. "Dear God," I said to myself, "how similar this man's sentiments are to those of our faith, and how easy it is to marry the two together! We arrived here naked and, for as long as we remained innocent, our nudity remained agreeable. Only sin has given us this horror of ourselves and, having soiled our soul before God, made us unbearable to ourselves. To see these people, you would think that Adam had not sinned in them, and they are what we would have been but for that fatal Fall. Far from feeling any modesty or shame at appearing naked, they are proud of it above all else, and they cannot imagine how one could endure the slightest covering without admitting to deformity. What is true among us, that the ugly seek to disguise their deformity out of shame, is true among them of their bodies. The Australians hide nothing for fear of being considered to have something dirty and nasty to hide. We excuse our custom on the grounds of the emotions and urges that nudity arouses, but I have no doubt that, on reflection, such reasoning must be judged very weak.

"It is a fact of life that we are aroused by what is hidden from us and despise that which is freely given. A married man will see his wife's nudity and sleep with her for many nights without any reaction, whereas the sight of another woman will cause impulses that he can control only by doing himself considerable violence. It is proverbial that familiar things cause no emotion, whereas the unaccustomed causes surprise—excites and carries one away.[12] To begin with I was ashamed of my nakedness here, and for some

---

12. A central insight of modern communications theory.

time could not look innocently at others; but in time I became accustomed to it and so indifferent that I no longer even think about it. Now even the thought of clothes upsets me, and I could not endure them without revulsion. The fact that God made us naked is convincing proof that only a moral failing causes us to clothe ourselves, that because he gave us clothes as the mark of our disobedience, we cannot wear them without declaring ourselves criminals nor like them without glorifying the mark of our servitude and the sins that caused it."

Next we moved on to the question of avarice, of which I could see that he understood only the name; for he confessed to being quite unable to conceive why anyone should want to accumulate strange and useless things. All Australians have in abundance what they need for their upkeep; they do not know what it is to accumulate nor even to keep anything for the morrow. Their life could be considered a true image of natural contentment, showing that only our habit of living in the future makes us miserable.

As for ambition, he had a vague notion of it although not to the extent of being able to conceive of some men being above others. I told him that in our country we believed a multitude could not exist without order and that order presupposed the necessity of a leader to whom others had to submit. The old man, without going any further into the various forms of hierarchy among us, expounded a doctrine that I understood fairly well at the time but am unable now to relay with the force that he gave it. He implied that it is man's nature to be born free: that he cannot be subjugated without ceasing to be himself; that in subjection he sinks lower than the beast because beasts exist only to serve man, and captivity is as it were their natural state. A man cannot be born to serve another man, because a purpose must always be more noble than its effects.

He continued this brilliant argument by saying that to subject a man to another man was to subject him to his own nature, to somehow make him a slave of himself, which could not be done without contradiction and extreme violence. He proved that the essence of man consists in his liberty, and that to take this away from him, without destroying it entirely, was to make him live without his true essence . . . that, if one does manage to capture and bind him, he may lose the outward signs of liberty, but his inward liberty remains undiminished. Just as a stone loses nothing of its weight when it is raised or held (gravity reclaiming it with equal force as soon as it is released), so man endures his captivity only because it is imposed on him. As soon as that force ceases to operate he reveals what he is, and his glory lies in being able to choose death in preference to bondage. It is not that he does not often want to do what others desire, but he does not act then because told or commanded to do so. They very word *commandment* is odious to him, and he does only what reason dictates. His reason is the law, the rule, and his only guide.[13]

There is this difference, he went on, between true men and half-men: that all the thoughts and wills of the former, being perfectly unified, are the same, without any difference; it suffices to explain them once in order for them to be embraced without opposition, just as reasonable people follow a true path with pleasure once it is pointed out to them. But because half-men have only the rudiments of knowledge and reason, it necessarily happens that one will think one thing and another something else: that one will follow a path while another flees it, arguing and complaining incessantly. The proof of this is evident—he who only glimpses the truth cannot avoid the dangers of self-deception and confusion of issues.

This discussion had already lasted for at least four hours, and would have gone on much longer had it not been the hour for

---

13. Such arguments were later used against slavery.

public assembly. I entered the Hab with my mind full of the arguments I had heard, admiring the knowledge and under-standing of these people. The force of the man's arguments stunned me, and I spent the duration of the assembly in a kind of trance. It seemed that the scales had fallen from my eyes and that I was seeing things in a quite different way. Over the following week I was forced to make continual comparisons between what we are and what I was seeing here. I could not help admiring their behavior in comparison to all our shortcomings, and was ashamed to have to admit to myself how far removed we are from their perfection. "So," I wondered "could it be true that we are not fully human?" When the principles of our faith caused me to reject this thought, I mused, "and yet their maxims surpass not only our behavior but the whole of our natural morality; one could not imagine anything more rational and exacting than what seems to come quite naturally to them. This inviolable unity among them so that they do not even know what division is; this detachment from all goods without even knowing how one could love them; this inviolable purity of their relationships with each other so that they do not even know how children are produced; and finally this close attachment to reason that unites them all and causes them to do all that is right and necessary— these are the fruits of a people consumate in all that can be conceived of natural perfection, and if God deigned to further enlighten them with his grace, there is no doubt that this would be Paradise on earth.

Thus, when I had time to dwell on our imperfections in the light of such virtue; when our continual dissensions, quarrels, bloody wars between brothers, our insatiable greed to possess at all costs, and the shameful disorders of our sexual relations passed through my mind—in a word, when I was forced to admit that we are led by passion rather than by reason—then I confess I admired these people and hope that their example of a true man might one day puncture the vanity of those who, although claiming divine illumination, live worse than beasts, while others who profess only humanity can show such exemplary virtue.[14]

14. Much of this was omitted in 1692, especially the passages on nudity and freedom—an important early commentary on missionary and other reports, as noted.

CHAPTER SIX

The Australians' Religion

The most sensitive and hidden subject of all among the Australians is religion. It is a heinous crime to speak of it, whether for or against. Only their "mothers" in giving them their first understanding, instill in them some idea of the Haab or Incomprehensible. This force is believed to be everywhere and is honored accordingly. But the youth are taught to worship it without speaking of it and to believe that they could not discuss its qualities without offending it, from which it follows that their great religion is not to talk about religion.[1]

Because I have always had the greatest respect for religion, I lived there for a long time extremely worried that there seemed to be no cult and no mention of God. I mentioned my anxiety to Suains who, after hearing me out, led me by the hand up a garden path and said graciously, "Is it possible that you could be more

---

1. Such ideas were associated notably with the Inca cult of the sun, well known by Foigny's time through the *Commentarios reales* of the Inca-Spaniard Garcilaso de la Vega. French editions appeared in 1633 and 1670, by which time deism was also reported from Asia and China, and Spinozist ideas were spreading in Europe itself (see Spink 1960, Vernière 1954). Most of this chapter was omitted in 1692.

human in your knowledge of the Haab than in your other behavior? Tell me all you know, and I shall do the same." I was delighted by this chance to communicate some understanding of my beliefs, and speculated that God might have led me to this land to serve him by enlightening this people who lack nothing in the world except knowledge of him.

I explained, as well as I could, that we had two sorts of knowledge of God in our countries: the one natural and the other metaphysical. Nature teaches us the existence of a sovereign being, the author and conservator of all things. "This truth impresses itself on me," I said, "whether I look at the earth, the heavens, or myself. As soon as I am aware of works that could only have been created by a superior force, I am obliged to recognize and adore a being that could not itself have been made but was their maker. And when I consider myself, I am convinced that I could not exist without a beginning and that in consequence the trail leads back to a first being that, having had no beginning itself, must be the origin of all the others. When my reasoning has led me to this first principle, I conclude without difficulty that it cannot be limited because limits necessarily imply production and dependence."

The old man did not let me continue. He interrupted and remarked with considerable satisfaction that if my kind were able to formulate such a concept, we could not be without the most solid understanding. "I have always thought just as you do," he added, "and although it would take an extremely long detour to verify this approach, I am convinced that it can be done. I can see, however, that great cycles of evolution over thousands of centuries must have made what we now see very different from its beginnings. But my mind does not allow me to conceive of such an eternity or total production, without the action of a sovereign being that would be its great architect and supreme moderator.

"To let your imagination wander among millions of billions of evolutions and reduce all that we see to a few chance encounters having no other principle than local movement and the collision of atoms is to involve yourself in difficulties that can never be resolved. It is to risk committing an execrable blasphemy; to give to the creature what can belong only to the Creator and, consequently, to repay with gross ingratitude that to which we owe all that we are, denying that it is the principle of all being and trying to ignore it even though it is manifest in all its effects. Even if one agreed that all these productions were eternal—considering that the opposite view is at least as likely, if not more so—one would willfully commit a sin by abandoning the eternal in favor of bodies without feeling and incapable of any intelligence.

"I mean that in arguing against the existence of a Being of beings, one would open oneself up to a charge of criminal fraud and deserve disgrace and punishment. On the other hand, in siding with this Being, one cannot help doing its will; one cannot fall into error, but must find oneself in its favor. In a word, this hypothesis is most plausible, and one can only do well by following it, whereas the alternative is dangerous and cannot be followed without committing a blasphemy. This reasoning caused us, about forty-five revolutions ago, to suppress all speculation about the Supreme Being: to simply teach that it is the foundation of all our principles and not allow anyone to think otherwise."

I listened to the man's oracles with the utmost attention; the elegance and measured pace of his words impressed my heart as much as my ears. Seeing that he was about to move on to some new question, I added that, even if one allowed that the existence of these productions were eternal,[2] one could never prove that they had made the world what it is by arguing from the principle that "like produces like"; these atoms, having no difference among themselves but number and plurality, would have been able to generate at most only further masses of like quality.

---

2. Sadeur here repeats almost verbatim the words of Suains, indicating their fundamental agreement at this stage of the dialogue.

"What causes difficulty for certain minds," he rejoined, "is the great abstractness of this Being of beings, which no more reveals itself than if it did not exist. But that proves to be a weak argument; many of us maintain that it is so far above us as to be manifested only in its effects. If its ways were "revealed," I would find it difficult to believe that they belonged to it, given that a universal Being can only act universally and without favor." I replied, "But if this great Sovereign is as you say, how can it be that you do not establish any religion to honor him? We who recognize him have set hours for his worship; we have our prayers to invoke him, hymns to glorify him, and his commandments to keep."

"You speak quite freely of the Haab, then," he said. "Yes, of course," I replied, "and these are our finest and truest discourses: our finest because there can be nothing more agreeable than to talk about him on whom we depend for life and death and our truest because this subject above all others can inspire us with respect and faith." "Nothing could be more praiseworthy," he responded, "but are you all of like mind as to the identity of this Incomprehensible Being?"[3] "There are some," I admitted, "who do not recognize his sovereign perfection in quite the same ways." "Speak positively and clearly," he urged sharply. "Are you united in your concept of this primary principle?" Upon which I had to confess that our minds were considerably divided in their views, causing much conflict and hatred and giving rise to wars, murder, and other unfortunate consequences.

The old sage replied very ingenuously that if I had replied in any other way, he would have abandoned the dialogue and despised me because it necessarily follows that in discussing something incomprehensible, one will speak with great diver-

---

3. This was the classic question put to missionaries by "savage sages" and formed a model for works such as Foigny's or, later, Baron La Hontan's *Dialogues with a Savage* (1703). It inspired early libertarian thought in general.

sity. "One would be foolhardy to try to ignore a first principle, but one would have to be infinite like the thing itself to be able to speak infallibly about it, given that it is assumed to be incomprehensible. From which it follows that as soon as one ventures into the subject, and yet can only speak of it by means of conjecture, one will be the more satisfied the less one approaches the truth. And because one is more than blind in such speculations, it is to be expected that each will think his own thoughts. It is reason that prevents us from thinking about it: we are convinced that one cannot speak about it without falling into error. Our assemblies in the Hab are for the purpose of recognizing and worshiping it, but with the inviolably observed rule that no word be spoken and each be left with his own private thoughts on the matter. This practice ensures that we are always united and devout when its name is mentioned, which would be impossible if we were at liberty to discuss it, just as surely as one courts death in climbing a cliff-face.

"I have taken note," he added, "of what you said about the dissensions and catastrophes caused by your differing systems of knowledge, and you must agree that yours is inexcusable behavior. The common doctrine as to this first cause ought to be what binds us together, in the same way that it is the common cause of our origin. Given that one cannot talk for long without differences arising, you must be aware that when these differences cause quarrels and wars, one abuses the common father on the very point that should provide unity. How can you imagine that you are pleasing him when you destroy each other on the pretext of doing his will? He can only be known as a universal cause to which everything belongs in the same way, one that grants movement and rhythm to all individuals and arranges everything according to his will. Do you not then abuse his goodness in butchering each other simply because some believe they know him better than others?"

I replied that such behavior could be explained by the zeal of each group to extend its religion, which various individuals believed to be so good that they shord it up with personal revelations and confirmed it with miracles, taking God to be the author of these. This amazed him beyond all measure, and as he could not reconcile it with the appearances of reason that he had noticed previously, he said in a menacing tone, "Perhaps it is rather that in trying to please me you have deceived me, and misrepresented your people as well? Is it possible that with the intelligence you have already displayed, these 'revelations' can be believed?" I protested that I was indeed being sincere and that although I was delighted to please him, I would not do so at the expense of the truth. I added that it was not a single people that held these diverse beliefs; but that the European situation was as if each seizain believed differently from the next, so that they would despise each other, quarrel, hate, and often fight each other.

"But are they not capable," he pursued, "of reflecting on their behavior? Using the knowledge you say they have of the infinite goodness and wisdom of the divine Being, can they not see that he would not sanction these contradictions? Does it not occur to them that in their mutual differences with their brothers both sides might be wrong? What great certitude is it that exempts them from a proper degree of scepticism?" I replied that they were thoroughly convinced that God had revealed himself to certain of their number and had commanded that these be listened to and obeyed as his representatives—not, however, through the use of force, but by anticipating each person's death in order to recompense the believers and punish the unbelievers.

"But how can you believe," he went on, "that the Haab has spoken to some and not to others? Where does this judgment come from that he prefers to bestow his enlightenment on some rather than on others?" I said that the miracles they had performed were proof positive that God was master of his will and could do as he pleased and that his creatures' place was to worship and submit to him. He asked me how it could be known that these revelations were genuine, given that others of contrary beliefs did not accept them; to which I answered that they were passed from father to son.

"If that be so," he responded, "then the religion they observe is founded neither on the word of God (for they dispute among themselves whether or not it is his), nor on any miracles authorizing it; as none of those believing them can claim to have observed them, whereas others who do not believe reject them as superstitions; so that in the end, it has no other foundation than the credulity of those most easily persuaded." I replied that there were very few who did not believe the same revelations; but that the diversity of religions arose from the differing interpretations put on them.

"Let us pass over this subject," he said. "You only get into difficulties and fall from error into error by trying to explain too much. If all that you describe were feasible, you would be portraying your people as having their way enlightened only to reveal inevitable precipices where they must fall into misfortune. What you say proves that they can conceive of a first Being only by making him partial, his revelations obscure and in need of interpretation, by considering him indifferent to the disputes waged in his name, and by making him appear cruel for destroying in the end those who work hardest to please him, should their efforts be misplaced. All these practices of yours are mere chicanery, unworthy of a Supreme Being that can act only with consummate prudence and wisdom.

"As for us, we know the primacy and ultimate sovereignty of this first Cause. We find by our reasoning that because all creatures are equally his, he sees them all with the same eye and the same affection. In fact, we realize that we are of so little importance to him that we are quite unworthy of his attention.

The individual destiny that you cite as an ultimate sanction amounts merely to the proof of one obscure thing by another that is even more obscure.

"We still need to determine whether there is any difference between the corpses of a man and any other animal; for the end result is the same and cannot give rise to any metaphysical distinction. The question can be approached, if at all, only by way of conjecture. Certainly we see that a living man is more vivacious than an animal, but this is not sufficient to convince one that he retains any such advantage after death. Because animals, which vary among themselves, are all equal in death, I can arrive at no positive judgment as to the being of man after death from the fact of his superiority during life. There are, however, some among us who make too great a distinction between man and brute and cannot accept that the former dies just like the latter. But when we ask them to explain the difference, they hesitate, get lost among their thoughts, and are unable to oblige. For to say that this 'supplement' remains with the body in the earth is to make it a superfluous supplement, whereas to say that it withdraws leaves the problem of assigning a place where it might go, unless it returns into other bodies . . . but these notions are shrouded in numerous difficulties that cannot be resolved."

The hour of the Hab then made us leave off, and I spent it going over my recollections of what he had explained. Finding in it problems beyond the reach of my mind, I thanked Providence for giving me another kind of enlightenment, clearer and more certain, and for having made me know that as my creator and savior, it had endowed me with a certain immortal soul that would share its glory. I was not at all sure whether I should reveal to Suains the faith we have in a God who died and was resurrected for our salvation. At last, after a long struggle, I concluded that it would only be casting pearls before swine to attempt such a discussion. Knowing his temper and his mind, I was convinced that he would tie me up in innumerable difficulties and make us out, in his customary way, to be imbeciles.

I remembered the words of the apostle that "the preaching of the cross is to them that perish foolishness; but unto us which are saved it is the power of God."[4] And certainly the knowledge I have acquired of this nation leads me to conclude that it is all the more incapable of supernatural knowledge for believing impossible or "incomprehensible" what it cannot understand. It is true that it is capable of a great deal, that reason is its guide and would make it incomparable if joined to faith. But this same reason that raises it so far above others in natural knowledge drags it down beneath all others in that it does not know its own salvation. You could say that its science serves only to blind it, that the liveliness of its wit and the blithe manner in which it revels in reason must, while making it a miracle on earth, be a curse to it in eternity.

I leave it to the learned to judge their practice of not speaking of God in any way and to find traces of it in Classical Antiquity. What I can say for certain is that it holds them in admirable respect and unity regarding things divine.

They often found me on my knees on the ground with my hands joined and my eyes raised heavenwards, and because they were astonished by this posture, my old sage asked me one day what I was trying to do. When I said that I was praying to God, he replied that he did not see how one could pray to him without insulting him, reasoning approximately thus: "To pray to or invoke the Haab necessarily supposes that he either does not know what we want or does not wish to grant it and, furthermore, that we could influence him by our importunity or, at least, that he is indifferent and could be drawn to our side. To think the first is blasphemy; to think the second is impiety; to think the third is sacrilege. It is blasphemous to think that he who comprehends all could be unaware of something; and one cannot without

4. St. Paul's First Epistle to the Corinthians (1:18).

impiety imagine that he could be made to will something he did not already will, for that would be to believe that one can change him and make him will something other than the best. We cannot think otherwise without abandoning our first principle of reason, which teaches us that the Haab cannot err and cannot will other than the good. This truth is so clear to us that it forms one of our first rules of logic.

"Furthermore, one could not ask anything of the Haab without rashness or ignorance: rashness, firstly, in that one would be supposing one's sentiments to be more worthy than his and would seek to divert the course of his conduct and make him act against his intentions. For one asks either for what one believes to be the best or for what, although not the best, suits one best. If one believes it to be the best, it is both presumptuous and futile to ask for it. Secondly, it is a display of ignorance to seek without reflecting whether or not it is the best that one is seeking. For these reasons, we expect anything and seek nothing; we accept all that happens to us without repugnance, fully convinced that it must be intended to be so even if it appears to us contrary and irritating."

I replied that it was believed among us that we were obliged to pray, and that at least when dying we ought to ask for God's mercy. I deliberately put forward this notion to find out his sentiments, but he only said, with his customary alacrity, that my response contained so many difficulties that he did not understand it and asked me to clarify it. I said that in dying we passed from one world to another where we were placed in accordance with the will of God.

"Changing worlds," he replied, "presupposes two worlds, and to make such a change necessarily supposes a voyage. You claim that having died—that is to say, having become incapable of motion—one makes this voyage with even greater motion than one had when alive. You claim two contradictory things: a living being that cannot travel to the other world and a dead one that can. You give more movement to the dead than to the living. At least think logically about what you are claiming."

I objected that I had not used the expression "other world" in the literal sense, of another place separate from the universe, but only to mean a form of existence quite other and different from the present one . . . that when I referred to "changing worlds" I never imagined that my proposition would be taken to mean all of us or a material journey.[5] I added that we were accustomed to using this manner of speaking to signify the separation of our principal part, which we call the soul and which, in distinguishing us from the animals, makes us creatures of reason, and that one would have to be worse than stupid to imagine that the body itself did not change back into earth, whereas our certitude was that what makes us rational beings, upon detaching itself from its bodily housing, becomes free and is carried in an instant to the place assigned to it by God, according to the quality of its actions in life.

"So you believe," he said, "that we become Habis,[6] that is to say, angels, in dying; that in ceasing to exist, we become more perfect than while alive. But you are too confused to explain your point. Our life being only a succession of movements, it follows that its cessation is only a cessation of movement, and that, far from being able to act more perfectly once dead, we are then incapable of action because we no longer have movement."

I begged him to look at it from my point of view and to answer more positively because I was attempting to draw a very considerable distinction between our selves and our souls, which are only parts of ourselves. "But," he rejoined, "when you claim

5. Foigny may be suggesting here the sort of meaning utopian "displacement" had for him and others in an age still dominated by theological notions.

6. This term, rhyming with the French *habits* (clothes), may further allude to arguments of the time over the significance of clothing and nudity. Ronzeaud (1990, 130) offers alternative interpretations: the Hebrew *nabi,* a man inspired by God: or again Habia, the name of a priestly patriarch.

that this part moves, acts, and is happy or sad, it must be either the same or not the same as before. If it is the same, you cannot condemn my reasoning. If it is not the same, then you have expressed yourself poorly in saying that at death one is placed according to one's works." I said that it was the same in part. "Very well," he went on, "and that means the most noble part, which should thus be taken for the whole." I had to grant him this. "So I am right," he continued, "to insist on what you were unable to reconcile, in claiming that you die and at the same time that, instead of dying, you live more perfectly than before. The ideas you have tried to explain represent you as a precious entity encased in crude matter, which death, far from harming, actually serves by freeing it from that corruption. It follows that what you call death is your perfection and not your destruction. Or rather that to die, according to you, is not to die but to cease dying, which cannot be because it is both dying and not dying together, ceasing to be and being more perfectly, being destroyed and existing more fully than before."

I realized that I could only scandalize and irritate the man by persisting in trying to instruct him in our beliefs. I begged him to excuse my weakness and to explain his thoughts on the matter. This he did in such lofty terms that I could scarcely take in what he said although as I listened I caught the drift of his propositions. As far as I can remember, he entered into the doctrine of a "universal genius" that is dosed out to each individual and conserved, when the animal dies, until such time as it is communicated to another one, or (to explain it more fully in terms of their philosophy) a principle that is extinguished in death without, however, being destroyed, awaiting only the occasion to be re-kindled in a new housing, according to the quality of its "fire."[7]

7. In other words, metempsychosis, a common feature of materialist systems such as that of the Australians or its ancient (Stoic, Pythagorean, or Heraclitean) models.

CHAPTER SEVEN

The Australians' Sentiments about This Life

𝕀 should mention three things regarding the Australians' attitudes about this life: the first concerns its beginnings; the second, its conservation; and the third, its end.

I have already touched on the manner in which their young come into the world, but because it is a central topic of this story and would cause no end of amazement if its implications were fully understood, I think it appropriate to dwell a little further on the matter. They have such an aversion to any mention of their beginnings that when, about one year after my arrival, I broached the subject in the company of two brothers, they suddenly turned their backs on me as if I had committed a horrible crime. One day I told this to my old philosopher, who, after admonishing me, entered into a long explanation to the effect that children arrive in their entrails in the same way that fruits grow on trees.[1] But on seeing that none of his propositions made any impression on

---

1. Mystical propositions of an ideally vegetal and/or hermaphrodite existence had been parodied in Hellenistic utopias and that of Lucian, as mentioned.

76

me and that I could not help smiling, he left me without finishing, indicating that my incredulity arose from a corruption of my mind.[2]

It also happened that during the first six months of my stay the brothers' ardent caresses caused me to experience a certain physical effect, which some of them noticed and were so scandalized that they would have nothing further to do with me. This eventually earned me the hatred of them all, as I have mentioned, and my death would have been certain without the special protection of the old man. I have to admit that in the thirty-two years that I have been among them I have never been able to find out how they procreate. Their "parts" are very small and give no signs of producing the monthly discharge common to women when not pregnant. Their children are unaffected by conditions such as scarlet fever, measles, or chicken pox to which European children are subject.

As soon as an Australian has conceived, he quits his apartment and goes to the Heb where he is received with great congratulations and supported without having to work. They deliver their "fruit" in a certain raised spot where they simply part their legs and allow the infant to drop onto a bed of Balf leaves. The mother then takes her child, rubs it with the leaves and gives it to suck, without losing any blood or appearing to suffer in any way. They do not use swaddling clothes, diapers, or cradles. The mother's milk is so nourishing that it satisfies the youngsters for two years and their excrements so minimal that one could say they effectively produce none at all.

They usually speak at eight months, walk at one year, and are weaned at the age of two. They begin to reason at three with the aid of some games I cannot explain. As soon as their mother has left them, the first master of the first band begins teaching them

2. 1692: "of my morals."

the elements.[3] They remain in his charge for three years before passing into that of their second master, who teaches them writing; this continues for four years, and so on, up to the age of thirty-five when they are all fully educated in the natural sciences without any difference of capability among them. Having thus completed their formation, they are ready to become lieutenants, that is, to take the place of those wishing to quit the world.

I mentioned their demeanor in chapter 5, and in truth, it consists of a gentleness and seriousness that are difficult to find in Europe. Their health is so perfect that they never know illness. I think their robust constitution comes from both the manner of their birth and the excellent food that they eat in moderation. Our ills have the opposite origins: we are conceived in passion and live on food lacking in nourishment and, therefore, often eaten in excessive quantities. Our parents usually pass on to us whatever faults they have acquired from their disordered life. If gluttony is their vice, they pass it on in such measure that we fill ourselves with poisons, which must be purged if we are to survive. If they are excessively passionate, the poxy signs of their quest show up on our bodies. In a word, they magnify in us what they themselves are; they cannot do otherwise. Their ardor makes us behave like animals in rut, and their irritability inflames us with anger.

The Australians are exempt from all these passions because their parents do not suffer from them and so cannot pass them on. Because they have no principle of dynamism, they live in a sort of indifference without any other movement than that dictated by reason. The same could be said about their food. We Europeans, although often harmed by the defective foods we eat, take two or three times as much as we need for our nourishment, from which follow our fevers, colds, stomach upsets, and many conditions unknown to the Australians. The latter are preserved from

3. 1692: "elements of reading."

all such ills by the great richness of their fruits and their admirable habit of eating only as much as they need. Far from reveling in eating and in sumptuous banquets, they steal away and eat in private, considering this a shameful animal function from which man should abstain as much as he is able. This means, too, that they experience so seldom the "call of nature" that they scarcely produce any excrement in a week.

They all agree that life is only an agitation, a trouble, and a torment. They are convinced that what we call death is their release and that the greatest possible good for any creature is to return to it as soon as possible. This way of thinking means that they live not only with indifference to life but even with a desire to die. As soon as they noticed that I showed some fear of death, they were confirmed in the suspicion that I could not be human because I lacked the true principles of reason. My old sage spoke to me about it several times, and here are more or less the reasons he gave:

"We are different from the animals in that their understanding does not penetrate to the bottom of things, and they draw consequences only from what is apparent on the surface. It follows that they flee their destruction as the greatest of evils and are concerned with their conservation as the greatest good, not seeing that this is a futile struggle and that, because their death is inevitable, to delay it is only to prolong their struggle. To reason profoundly, we must consider ourselves to be in a state of misery: in the first place because our actions are tied to a heavy body, and the more we act, the more we suffer. We can only cease to suffer in ceasing to act, so that, frankly speaking, to desire to live is to wish to burden oneself, whereas to seek death is to aspire to rest and release from suffering, this being all the more true in that we must necessarily die and delaying it can only cause us greater ills.

"The thought that nothing is dearer to us than ourselves can only—because we are obliged to view ourselves as perishing—

cause us to languish rather than live and to admit that it would be better not to exist at all than to exist only to be conscious of our mortality. Self-preservation is useless because we must die, and delay can only serve to increase our regrets. The sight of our perfection causes further torment for it can only be regarded as a temporary possession that has cost a great deal to create, only to be suddenly lost. In the end, all that we see within and outside of ourselves appears to us nothing more than a burden and an insult."

I said that this reasoning seemed to me to prove too much. To give it its full weight I would have to feel sad about knowing of something that transcended me, which would be all the more reprehensible in that rightness of judgment consists of accepting one's condition and rejecting thoughts that serve only to afflict one—especially when there is no remedy.

"There is some reason in what you say," he went on, "but it is weak in two ways: firstly, concerning your suspension of judgment and secondly, in the matter of being able to love oneself without hating one's destruction.[4] It is a great weakness to be able to live without being constantly aware of one's imminent destruction. It is an even greater one to fear what one knows must happen. But it is an extreme weakness to invent means of avoiding what one knows to be inevitable. To be able to exist without seeing death is to live without knowing oneself. For death is inseparable from ourselves, and to see ourselves fully is to see nothing but mortal flesh. To fear death is to admit two contradictory things because fear presupposes a doubt as to what will happen, whereas we know indubitably that death must occur. It is even worse to seek palliatives to deflect that reality, which we know to be impossible."

---

4. 1692: *le néant* (the void, nothingness), possibly a reference to the principle that "nature abhors a vacuum," as set out by Descartes (*Principes philosophiques.* 2:16). Cf. Descartes 1971, 205.

I replied that we could justifiably fear not death but its approach, and that the palliatives were useful, at least in staving off the latter for a while. "Very well, he went on, "but can you not see that because it is all the same in the end, to delay death only causes a series of troubles, anxieties, regrets, and irritations, and that it serves only to burden one and increase one's misery?"

I remarked that these arguments would carry much more weight among the Europeans than in their country, where they barely knew what it was to suffer, whereas the life of Europeans was a veritable vale of tears. "What!" he exclaimed, "have you other infirmities other than those of being mortal and knowing that you are dying?" I assured him that we were often at death's door several times before finally dying and that death only came to Europeans in the form of illnesses that struck them down and ultimately overcame them. This notion was a mystery to him, and he could only interpret it in terms of the fighting among ourselves that we had previously discussed. When I tried to explain about our gouts, migraines, and colics, I could see that he understood nothing of what I meant. To make him understand my proposition I had to explain in detail some of the illnesses we suffer from, and when he had heard me, he rejoined, "Is it possible that one could love such a life?" I replied that we not only loved it but did everything possible to prolong it. This gave him fresh reason to accuse us of insensitivity or of intolerable eccentricity, on the grounds that our being certain of finally dying, watching ourselves dying through suffering, yet prolonging our lives at the price of continual lassitude and not seeking a prompt death amounted to behavior inconceivable to a mind capable of reason.

"Our sentiments keep us far removed from such a policy," he added. "As soon as we come to know ourselves, we love ourselves and consider ourselves necessarily the victims of a higher cause that takes pleasure in destroying us. So we thoroughly despise our lives, regarding them only as transitory possessions. The time that we have them is charged to our account in that they only cause us to regret what are to be taken from us even more casually than they were given. Finally, we get sick of living because we do not dare form the intimate attachments to ourselves that we could: just as he who had a charming room for a time would fear to give it his heart so as not to suffer too much when the time came to leave it."

I pointed out nature's lesson, that being was preferable to nothingness: that it was better to live, were it only for a day, than not to live. But he replied, with a force that I shall explain, "It is necessary to distinguish two aspects of being: one that is existence in general and does not perish and the other that is individual existence and does. The first is better than its absence, and that is absolutely what should be intended when one says that being is preferable to nonbeing; whereas the second is often worse than its absence, especially if knowledge of it only serves to make us miserable."

I countered that if being in general were better than nonbeing, it followed that being in particular was worth more than its negation. But he argued otherwise by invoking the example of the state I had arrived in. "Tell me truthfully," he said, "when you were alone in those places you spoke of, surrounded on all sides by death, were you able then to believe that your life was a boon? Did you value it more than its opposite? Is it not true that your perceptions only made you more miserable so that you would have preferred to be insensible to your plight? So you are wasting your time in insisting that self-knowledge is necessarily a good, because knowledge that afflicts is not a good but an evil to be avoided. It is from this principle that our real misery follows in the world and our great revulsion at having to remain in it.

"We Australians take account of what we are and of what we should be: we know that we are by nature noble, perfect, and worthy of eternal life. We see that, notwithstanding this excellence, we are dependent on a thousand and one inferior elements for our existence and subject to the whims of a sovereign will that has made us only to change us when and how it likes, and that demonstrates its power as much in destroying as in creating us. That is what we cannot accept, and what makes us prefer to cease existing rather than be so exalted, only to know that we must eventually be treated worse than the most wretched and abject of creatures. We consider ourselves as persons raised up only to be cast down and treated worse than beasts, and, indeed, one would have to be more insensible than the latter not to be aware of this.

"Our ancestors were so convinced of this truth that they eagerly sought to die. Then, as our lands became depopulated, reasons were found to persuade those remaining to spare themselves for a time: it was argued that such a vast and fine continent should not be wasted, that we were the ornament of the universe and should seek to please the Sovereign Being in all respects. Some time later, to fill all the vacant places each individual was required to present between one and three infants to the Heb. Then when the country was repopulated, about one hundred and fifty years ago, this obligation was eased to a requirement that no one be allowed to seek the great repose until he had presented a lieutenant. If he lacked a natural son, he had to find one from elsewhere. It is only twenty-nine years since an assembly of the Hab ruled that one could not seek permission to leave until he had reached the age of one hundred or had some wound that visibly weakened or disfigured the body."

At this point two other brothers joined us, to my annoyance, for the old philosopher had never seemed as keen to instruct me as he was then. I thought at some length about what he had said, and saw that great consolation could be brought to them. If this people could enjoy the enlightenment that faith brings to us, it would be as happy as it was now sad through being deprived of it. Their sadness at seeing themselves obliged to cease to exist would be turned into incredible joy if they were aware, like us, that death comes not to destroy us but to exempt us from dying and raise our being to eternal fulfillment. If their grief at knowing of their necessary death makes them wish to cease to exist and even that they never had existed, then knowing of an afterlife, and that the transition to it was intended to glorify their existence, would crown their perfection.

To tell the truth of my attitude toward this policy of the Australians in relation to life, I do not know whether it should be attributed rather to a disdain for the shortness of life and to their high opinion of themselves, or to a certain intellectual prowess that they are very keen to display in all things. I have noticed that their desire to be considered intelligent is such that they take pains to excel in this, and make a point of embracing anything proposed to them that conforms better to reason. Thus, perhaps, having heard that the hallmark of the superior mind is to despise this life and to face death with resolute courage,[5] they have acquired and adopted this opinion as a principle.

There is no assembly of the Hab where twenty or thirty of them do not seek permission to return to the great repose, and there are few where it is not granted to someone when the reasons he gives are accepted. When permission is granted, he presents his lieutenant, who must be at least thirty-five years old; the company receives the latter with joy and gives him the name of the old man who wises to die. Then he is told of all the great deeds of his namesake, and assured that he is expected to prove just as worthy a citizen. When this ceremony is completed, the old man steps gaily up to the table, which is laid with Balf fruits, and calmly eats up to eight of them. After the first four he becomes abnormally uninhibited and performs all sorts of antics such as prancing about and telling tall stories; the brothers take no notice of these because they know they are the product of a mind losing its reason. Then two more fruits are offered to him, which

5. As in ancient Stoic doctrines and the contemporary deist or libertine ideas largely based on them, which Foigny thus compares to orthodox theological positions. This and the previous paragraph were (significantly) omitted in 1692.

derange his mind completely, and he is led by his lieutenant and another to the place he has chosen and prepared. There a further two fruits are administered, and he falls asleep for good. Finally, having secured the place, the others return to the Hab and declare that they ardently hope to enjoy as happy an ending.

That is how Australians live and die.

CHAPTER EIGHT

The Australians' "Exercises"

The Australians count their year from the first point of the Capricorn solstice,[1] which they determine by the shadow of a needle set against a northfacing wall. When this reaches its lowest point, the end of the old year and the beginning of the new is heralded throughout the land.

From this solstice to the March equinox, they count a Sueb, or "month," and from the March equinox to the June solstice is another month; a third lasts until the other (autumnal or September) equinox, and the fourth completes the year to the return of the Capricorn solstice. Thus they have only four months in their year. They call Suem what we call weeks, and have as many of them as there are moons, and no more; each week ends when a moon cycle is completed. They divide the days, which they call Suec, into three parts: Sluec, or morning; Suecz, or midday; and Spuec, or evening. They attach no importance to the night, other than as a time spent in fruit-induced sleep. Only their night guards are then awake until relieved by others who wake up at the appointed time, according to the amount of fruit they have eaten.

1. Around 22 December.

Sluec lasts from 5:00 A.M. until 10:00 A.M., Suecz until 3:00 P.M., and Spuec until 8:00 P.M. One of these periods is devoted to the Hab and to the sciences; another to work, and the third to public "exercises." They go to the Hab for five days at a time. The order they observe is that on one day the first quarter spends its Sluec there, the second quarter its Suecz, and the third its Spuec; on the following day the fourth quarter spends its Sluec there, followed by the fifth quarter during Suecz and the sixth quarter during Spuec. The day after that the seventh quarter, and then the eighth, ninth, and so on, take their turns in the Hab so that on the sixth day the first quarter has its turn again, not in the Sluec or morning but the Suecz.

Thus there can be seen in the Hab at any time at least four hundred persons, not counting those of the Hebs who accompany their quarter. They spend one-third of the day there without uttering a single word at a distance of one pace from each other and so engrossed in their own thoughts that nothing can distract them. I have learned that in earlier times they used to make certain outward signs accompanied by grimaces and contortions of the limbs, but it had been deemed wise to ban these entirely as being unworthy of the human mind.

On days not spent in the Hab, they are obliged to go to the Heb to discuss the sciences, which they do so methodically that I was delighted to see the diligence with which they take advantage of these periods. They propose, one after another, problems that have occurred to them and argue them with powerful reasoning. Then they respond to each other's problems, and at the conclusion of the debate, if something important has been discussed, they write it down in the public book, and one of them comments on it at length. If someone has found out something that displeases him or that he deems of public importance, he proposes it to the brothers, and they work out a more reasonable solution, having regard only for the national interest.

They spend the second third of their day in the gardens, which they cultivate with a skill unknown in Europe. They induce such a sweetness in their crops by feeding special mixtures to their roots that it would be considered miraculous in our lands. We have no royal chamber or hall as cleanly and richly maintained as their garden boulevards. In them art leads nature, producing such vivid images that they surpass those of our best paintings. What most surpasses comparison is that at first sight everything looks the same, but the closer one looks, the more diversity one discovers. It is, in truth, only a resemblance within continual diversity; if one sight is charming, the next will be ravishing. What crowns this perfection is that such effects are not momentary or limited to a few days' glory, as we expect in Europe, but last for whole years and, far from withering with time, become ever more lively, rich, and complex.

The last third of the day is devoted to three sorts of exercises that are extremely interesting. The first of these consists of demonstrating their latest inventions or of repeating earlier ones. But these periods rarely pass without some unheard-of new curiosity being proposed. The inventors of these gain the honor of being inscribed with their inventions in the Book of Public Curiosities, which is their equivalent of the highest honors among Europeans. In the thirty-two years I spent in the country, I witnessed more than five thousand of these, which would all have passed for prodigies among our most cultivated minds. Here are a few of the most recent that I can recall:

1. A brother appeared with a piece of very hard wood in his hand and gave the secret of softening it like molten wax and then liquefying it; then, adding to this liquid one ounce of seawater, he caused it to change after three hours into a twig bearing a beautiful living flower. When this was crushed and mixed with a kind of vitriol, a small animal the size of a cat emerged from it three hours later.

2. To a small amount of earth taken at random, moistened with a vitriolic salt, were added two spoonfuls of Balf juice. This mixture was blown on from a certain angle and then placed with some coverings in the sun. Two hours later a handsome titlike bird emerged although I noticed that it did not live long.

3. To one glassful of seawater was added six ounces of earth; into this was poured one-half spoonful of Balf juice, and then the mixture was wrapped in leaves and held under the brother's armpit for about six hours at the end of which time an amazing kind of small dog hatched out.

4. Having gathered half an ounce of dew, the brother mixed into it the nectar of a brilliantly red flower they have and left this to cook in the sun all day. The following day at sunrise, an incomparable living flower appeared.

5. After gathering one ounce of dew and mixing in two drops of seawater, a bubble was blown with this in the sun, which turned into a priceless little crystal bottle.

6. A leaf from any plant, washed in the morning with Balf juice, becomes harder than iron, whereas if washed again in the same liquid, it becomes white and soft like fine-quality paper. Indeed, that is what I am writing these lines on.

7. A fruit as large as our gourds was cut in two and emptied of its core, which was replaced with one glassful of seawater containing half an ounce of vitriol solution and a few drops of Balf juice. Then the two parts were put back together and left in the sun for two days, after which a harelike animal emerged and ran about pricking up its ears in astonishment. But it lived for only about three days as it had no fundament.

8. A certain oil extracted from the leaves of their garden root crops, when mixed with seawater and shaken by being turned on a small wheel, burns with a good flame although without producing any heat; it is commonly used for lighting.

9. A round stick rubbed with a small herb resembling our staghorn will prevent water from spilling onto the ground, or rather, the water will attach itself to it like iron to a magnet.

10. A wheel with four spokes ending in balls that extend and retract maintains perpetual motion. I noticed that this was produced by a suspended piece of wood that drew each ball toward the right and then pushed it leftward.

11. Some leaves were sewn together and rubbed twice with Balf juice with the addition of a few drops of sap pressed out of the leaves of the same tree. This produced a fabric more brilliant and polished than our gilded cloths.

12. If one rubs oneself with a mixture of seawater and juices from their garden fruits, one turns scarlet red; on rubbing oneself further with the same fluid, one becomes invisible for two hours.

The book of such wonders is as thick as one of the lives of the saints and is almost full.

Their second type of exercise is a sort of military arms— wielding contest. Some of these weapons resemble halberds, others our organ pipes. They handle the former with great agility although not with the dexterity I have seen in Europe. Their halberds are so thick and heavy that they can easily pierce six men at once. They are made of wood, but soaked in a solution of seawater and Balf juice that makes them both harder and lighter.

What I call organ pipes are sets of ten, twelve, or fifteen pipes with a certain kind of spring in their ends that, when released, can fire balls with sufficient force to penetrate five or six men at one blow. The skill with which they fire these makes it almost impossible to escape; one is hit before having time to duck or seek cover. They throw their halberds from thirty to forty paces with such accuracy that they can hit the same target ten or twelve times in a row. But their strength is even more amazing; they can carry six to seven hundredweight, and uproot trees that we could not even shake. I remember seeing one who, having skewered with his halberd four half-men (as they call us), carried them on one shoulder, two before and two behind.

Their third exercise of note is the handling of certain balls of three or four sizes. Some they throw into the air, others at targets, and some even at each other. The ones thrown into the air are launched four, five, or six at a time so as to collide at a target point. Those thrown at a target have to pass through a hole in its center, and they can succeed in doing this two or three times in a row.

What is remarkable about these contests is that they proceed in a happy, although serious and dignified, manner, without any disorders or upsets. The balls they throw at each other resemble our tennis balls[2] although perhaps softer and less dangerous. The skill of the thrower lies in hitting his opponent, who must prove his agility by dodging the balls. The enjoyment of watching them is so great that the people will put aside anything for the opportunity. Sometimes they dodge the ball with capering leaps; at other times they twist and turn with an agility unmatched by any comedian in our pats. When the adversary throws two, three, or four balls one after the other and the target bends to one, doubles up for another, catches and throws back the third and fourth with his hands (and sometimes his feet)—all of which takes place in an instant—the spectators' hilarity knows no bounds. Because the "aggressor" always throws accurately, the "prey" must either receive all the hits or display great skill in avoiding or deflecting them. I had been judged fairly clever and quick at such things in Portugal, but I certainly appeared clumsy among the Australians, and had I not excused my clumsiness on the grounds of the wounds I had received in my battle with the birds, I would have appeared and caused my race to appear dull and stupid.

2. Tennis balls were solid at the time.

CHAPTER NINE

The Australian Language and Education

They use the same three means of expression as are in use in Europe: gesture, the voice, and writing. Gesture alone is frequently used, and I have seen them spend several hours together without communicating in any way; for they hold to the great principle of economy of means of expression.

Thus they only speak when it is necessary to formulate a discourse or a long set of propositions. All their words are monosyllabic and their verb conjugations follow a similar methodology. For example, *af* means "to love," its present tense being *la, pa, ma* (I love, you love, he loves), *lla, ppa, mma* (we love, you love, they love). They have only one preterite or past tense: *lga, pga, mga* (I have loved, etc.), *llga, ppga, mmga* (we have loved, etc.), and a future tense, *lda, pda, mda* (I will love, etc.), *llda, ppda, mmda* (we will love, etc.). "To work" in Australian is *uf,* conjugated thus: *lu, pu, mu* (I work, etc.), *lgu, pgu, mgu* (I have worked, etc.).

They have no noun declensions nor even articles, and very few nouns at all. Things that are not compounded they express by a single vowel; those that are compounded, by the vowels that signify their main elements. They recognize only five simple elements, the most noble being fire, which they express by *a.* This is followed in descending order by air *(e)*, salt *(o)*, water *(i)*, and earth *(u)*.

To make individual distinctions they add consonants, of which they have many more than us Europeans. Each consonant signifies a quality modifying the substances signified by vowels: thus *b* means "clear," *c* means "hot," *d* means "unpleasant," *f*, "dry," and so forth. By following these rules, they manage to know immediately the meaning intended. Thus they call the stars *aeb*, a word explaining their composition of fire, air, and light; the sun is a *aab*. Birds are *oef*, signifying their solid, aerial, and dry qualities. Man is *uel* (aerial, terrestrial, and moist), and so on. The advantage of this system is that one becomes a philosopher as soon as one learns the first elements of speech. One cannot name anything in that country without at the same time making explicit its nature, which might indeed seem miraculous to those not aware of the secret method they use to this effect.[1]

If their way of speaking is admirable, their writing is even more so. They use only dots to express their vowels, and these are distinguished only by their location. There are five positions; the highest signifies *a*, the next one down *e*, and so on, thus:

    a

      e

        i

          o

            u

Although the distinction might seem obscure to us, their habitual use of this system makes it quite familiar to them. They

---

1. Linguistic cratylism, the idea of a *lingua humana* or universal language based on natural signs, was a feature of many such schemes by Wilkins, Dalgano, Leibniz, and others. It was a form of idealism closely related to utopianism both in theory and (since Godwin's *Man in the Moone* of 1638) in practice. It was greatly inspired by the Chinese example, as perceived by Jesuit missionaries. In the case of Leibniz, it was related to his work on differential calculus and related mathematical problems around

have thirty-six consonants, of which twenty-four are remarkable: they consist of strokes surrounding the dots, which have meaning according to the position they occupy. For example, *eb* ! means clear air; *oc·–* means hot water; *ix –·* is cold water; *ul ¡* , moist earth; *af ¡* , dry fire; *es !* , white air.[2] There are, as well, a further eighteen or nineteen consonants, but there is no European equivalent by which they could be explained.

The more one examines this system of writing, the more one uncovers its admirable secrets: thus *b* signifies clear; *c,* hot; *x,* cold; *l,* wet; *f,* dry; *s,* white; *n,* black; *t,* green; *d,* unpleasant; *p,* gentle; *q,* pleasant; *r,* bitter; *m,* desirable; *g,* bad; *z,* high; *h,* low. The consonant *i* means red; the diphthong *a-i,* peaceable. As soon as they utter a word they know the nature of what it signifies: thus to say that an apple is sweet and tempting, they write *ipm,* whereas a bad and unpleasant fruit is *ird.* I cannot explain all the other secrets that they understand and express in their writing.

Their verbs are even more mysterious than their nouns. For example, they write and say *af* for to love: *a* meaning fire, and *f* the dryness that love causes. They say *la* for I love, signifying the wetness found at the time of love; *pa,* you love, indicates the gentleness of the lover; whereas in *lla,* we love, the doubling of the consonant signifies the number of persons involved. *Oz* means to speak, *o* marking the saltiness with which our discourse should

1672–76, and to his coining of the term *monopsychite* for a being endowed with this universal spirit. See Pons 1932; Spink 1960, 248; Knowlson 1963; Cornelius 1965, 122ff.; Pellandra 1986; and Leibacher-Ouvrard 1989, 17–41.

2. Like Lachèvre (1968, 131n) I omit here some further baroque signs which Foigny added without any explanation or distinct punctuation, and can be approximated thus:

n ˅. t ⁄. d ! p ∟. q ⌐. r∟ . m ˥ g j. ve ,. ∟. j e . ∟. ⌐. ail

These were dropped from all subsequent editions. The last of them, *ail,* form the French word for garlic.

be seasoned, whereas *z* denotes the inflation and compression of the lungs that enables us to form words.

In teaching a child to speak, they first explain the meaning of all three elements so that as he joins them together he learns at the same time the essence and nature of all the things he will talk about. This is a great advantage both for individuals and for the public good because as soon as they can read (usually at three years), they already know the meaning attached to things by all the others. They can read perfectly by the age of ten and know all the subtleties of their language by fourteen; by twenty they are familiar with all the problems of philosophy. From then until the age of twenty-five they devote themselves to astronomy, in which they first learn about the revolutions of the stars that determine their calendar; secondly, how to identify these; and thirdly, about their qualities, which they do in a manner quite unlike that known in Europe. But because this is a purely philosophical matter, it would be inappropriate to enter into it here.

From twenty-five to twenty-eight years they study books of their history, and I believe it is in this area that they fall most heavily into ignorance and fantasy. It extends back over about twelve thousand revolutions of solstices. They teach that their origin was in the Haab or divinity, which breathed out three beings at once from which they are all descended. They have some old parchments that they believe to be eight thousand years old, in which their annals were recorded year by year in incredible detail. It requires a very penetrating and subtle mind to read and understand the first five thousand years of their history, and I have never been able to comprehend any of it. This consists of forty-eight books of prodigious size, which they keep in the Hab as sacred objects, to be touched only with the greatest respect, but the authority of these texts rests solely on the belief that their writers, being incapable of deception, were setting down an objective account of events in their time. If what they claim were true, there would be two-thirds again as many stars; the sun would be larger and the moon much smaller; the seas would have changed their shape over the course of time; and a thousand and one other unlikely events would have occurred.[3]

They place man's beginnings at the end of this five-thousand-year period, and their notions of them are totally ridiculous. According to their myth, an enormous amphibious serpent that they call Ams[4] threw itself upon a sleeping man and took its pleasure, without doing him any harm; whereupon the man awoke in such distress that he threw himself into the sea. The serpent, seeing his despair, plunged in after him and saved him from drowning, getting him to an adjacent island that no longer exists. There it won him over with caresses and marks of friendship and persuaded him to eat something.[5] A few months later the serpent noticed its fruit growing in the man and redoubled its efforts, and soon two hermaphrodite children were born. The serpent assiduously cared for the mother and its offspring, supplementing their regular diet of fruits with fish and small game.

As they grew, the two children began to show many signs of malice and brutality, causing the man such disappointment and sadness that he became depressed. The serpent noticed his grief and thought he was homesick, and after trying everything to cheer him up, it gave him to understand that it would help him and his children return, in the same way it had helped him arrive there. The man then dived into the water as much to test the serpent's word as for any other reason. But the serpent swam after him and supported him under his belly, bearing him back within

3. Whether these projections of scientific discoveries were prophetic or merely coincidental, they amount to a parody of both scientific method and religious miracles. As elaborated in the introduction, the Australians' materialist ethos was for Foigny a dystopia (see Vecchi 1986). These passages were omitted in 1692.

4. "Desirable white fire."

5. Again, this parody of the *Genesis* story was omitted in 1692.

two hours to his native land, after which it returned to its children.

The latter had by this time grown up and coupled with each other, producing many more offspring, which lived entirely by hunting and fishing like carnivorous beasts. Then, when the island became overpopulated, they invented ways of migrating to neighboring lands and spread their violent ways, with the resulting history of disorders that we know—this being our origin, according to the Australians.

When they reach thirty years of age, they are able to reason on any subject except that of the Haab and the Habes, that is, of the Divinity and of their annals. At about thirty-five they became lieutenants in the Hebs and live *en famille* with other brothers in apartments. After a further twenty-five years they can return to the Heb to teach, but they usually assume this role in accordance with their age sets unless some old man cedes the right of his own accord.

CHAPTER TEN

The Animals of the Southern Land

Everyone, however little versed in natural history, knows that animals differ between species as much as do the lands they inhabit. England, for example, has no wolves and rules a number of lands were serpents cannot live and the very earth of which, when transported elsewhere, causes them to die.[1] The wood of Ireland's forests hosts neither worms nor spiders. The Orcades[2] have no flies, and in Norway's Trondheim worms are unknown. Candia[3] has no venomous animals; and even if venom is transported to the Trinity Islands,[4] it loses its potency and is no longer fatal there.

1. Probably a satirical reference to Ireland, which is named in the following sentence (and in the 1692 edition, here).
2. The Orkney Islands.
3. An ancient name for Cyprus.
4. Cf. the Trinity Island at the beginning of chap. 3. Foigny may have based this, the Balf tree and so forth on an island of that name in the Antilles, mentioned in Alfonse (1559, 31). This work is central to the "Dieppe" enigma (cf. chap. 4, n. 20) concerning the way France apparently obtained secret Portuguese information about Australia early in the sixteenth century. See Fausett 1993. Whether or not there was this link with the region itself, Foigny was clearly interested in a current of French thought (largely fostered by Thévenot) which favored its exploration and colonization.

Again, it is well known that the largest creatures are not always the most dangerous. Our small vermin that the Australians find so incomprehensible, but which have no outstanding quality other than life itself, cause such problems in many parts of Europe that these often result in the plagues we know so well. Which is why I count it among the foremost advantages of Australian life that they are so completely free of any such insects as to be unable to believe what they are told about them, convinced as they are that life can only be supported by a body of human dimensions and capacities. None of our dirty, venomous, and irritating creatures are found in the entire expanse of their land, and I imagine that the robustness of their fruits is the result of the absence of such excrements. Thus too, their bodies are always vigorous, fresh, and free from the sores and bad breath that we suffer from in Europe. For the same reason, they lie and sleep on the ground quite readily and even with pleasure.

They have since ages past kept three sorts of domesticated animals. I could compare the smallest to our monkeys, except that their faces are not furry. Their eyes are protuberant, their ears fairly long, their mouths and noses of human form, their paws elongated and six-fingered, enabling them to handle and carry objects as easily as humans. They are very active and perform delightful tricks and are so tame that they die of hunger and sorrow if separated from people. Whenever they have an audience, they cannot resist putting on a show of capers, tricks, and antics of all sorts. Indeed, they are sustained more by the company of man than by food and will only eat in his presence. They have been banished from a number of seizains, however, because of their lively behavior, especially in the Hab where they created a continual distraction and profaned that sacred place. The only way to keep them from going there was to shut them in, but they were found dead on the brothers' return.

The second sort of animal bears some resemblance to a small pig but has hair as soft as silk and a longer snout; they are called

Lums.[5] They have a certain skill at ploughing the ground into regular furrows as neatly, if not more so, as our farmers with their ploughs, bullocks, and horses. Most conveniently of all, they begin, continue, and complete their rows without needing any human control. However, they too have been exterminated in the majority of seizains because of their excrement and because they are useful for only seven or eight days of the year; for the rest of the time they must be kept shut away so as not to make a mess, which they do as much for fun as out of necessity.

The third sort of animal could be compared to our camels were it not that their heads are more like that of a horse. Their backs have hollows, above which their sides rise in such a way that two men can easily ride in them. They are called Fuefs[6] and carry men in two ways: either by being mounted and ridden directly without a saddle—in this way eight men, the equivalent of at least twelve Europeans, can be carried—or, more conveniently, by being fitted with a kind of car seating four men. The animal is driven with a small stick that indicates to it the direction to take. However, it has been decided in our seizain that they should be destroyed not only because the giant carnivorous birds prey greedily on them but also because of the time spent maintaining, housing, and driving them. Such tasks are considered unworthy of a human being, who should at all times be engaged in elevated pursuits.

Apart from these animals, there are four sorts of birds that deserve our attention: the first are called Effs[7] and flit about like domestic fowls, being of similar size and brightly colored. They too are beginning to be banished from the seizains because of their droppings. Two further bird species resemble our siskins

---

5. "Wet/earth/desire" (changed in chap. 11 and in 1692 to "Hums," low/earth/desire, perhaps through casual transcription).

6. "Dry/earth/air/dry."

7. "Air/dry/dry."

and tits, although somewhat larger, and are so tame that they often have to be chased away. Their song is so sweet that one might even prefer it to our chamber music. They fly about with the brothers, following them everywhere, even into the Hab, where they instill a certain calmness of spirit with their warbling, which is called Pacd, or "song of joy." They eat only with the brothers and never rest except perching on them. They are able to smell the dreaded carnivorous birds from a great distance and warn the brothers by pecking them. In a word, they provide one of the most pleasant diversions for the people.

The fourth bird variety is the size of our bullocks, with a long, pointed head and a beak at least one foot long, harder and sharper than honed steel. They have true bull's eyes protruding from their heads; large ears; reddish and white feathers; necks by no means slender, but very thick; bodies about twelve feet long and four wide, with long tails of curved feathers; stomachs protected by feathers from blows and as hard as iron; and smallish feet, each ending in five frightful claws, capable of easily lifting a weight of three hundred pounds. These horrible creatures are called Urgs[8] and live on prey caught on land and at sea. At certain times of the year they invade the Australians' territories so ferociously that they will sometimes carry off ten, twelve, or fifteen of them in a single day. As soon as they have tasted human flesh, their greed for it is quickened, and then there is no ruse or strategy that they will not use to this end. Sometimes they form ambushes; sometimes they descend from the middle reaches of the atmosphere in droves of ten or fifteen,

8. "Earth/bitter/bad/salt." Foigny may have derived the name from the Latin *urgere* (to press, drive), the Greek *ergon* (work), and so on. As mentioned (introduction, n. 30), he could have had various sources for real reports of such creatures. Apart from the giant albatross or large Australian birds, there had been the giant Aepyornis on Madagascar (Bovetti-Pichetto 1978, 26) and the giant flightless moa that the Maoris had recently hunted to extinction in New Zealand.

braving the defenders' blows and rarely retreating without carrying off at least one man.

All things considered, the Australians are kept by these creatures alone from enjoying perfect natural bliss. Certainly, they have gone and still go to incredible lengths to destroy them, even to the extent of razing whole islands thirty or thirty-five leagues around with mountains one league high.[9] But whatever they have done and continue to try seems to make no impression on the birds. The islands are so numerous in these parts, even ten leagues out from the coast, and so rugged in form that it would be impossible to eliminate them all. Even if they were able to do so, there are still others farther away, so that their attempt would end up flattening the entire earth, as they have come to realize. But the following chapter will deal more fully with these creatures.

Apart from the animals I have mentioned, the Australians know a thousand secrets for creating new ones of all sorts, but because these cannot eat, they do not survive for long.

I should mention here that, far from eating animal flesh, they cannot even conceive how a man could do so. Their reasons are firstly, that such food is incompatible with humanity, which is far removed from such cruelty; secondly, that animal flesh is similar to that of men,[10] and eating the former could lead to eating the latter; thirdly, that its consumption is dangerous in that one cannot eat the flesh of an animal without acquiring its inclinations; fourthly, that the flesh of an animal is so adapted to its species that it could not nourish another that did not resemble it; fifthly, the very word *animal* is so repugnant to them that they would prefer not to exist at all rather than to engage with animality; sixthly, they have no notion of making a fire to cook

9. About one hundred miles around with mountains of eighteen thousand feet.

10. Contradicting the earlier assertion of Suains (cf. pp. 51–53). Such deliberate contradictions now appear, as the utopia begins to unravel.

with; and for a seventh reason, the antipathy between an Australian and the animal kingdom is such that he believes he would turn into an animal if he ate animal flesh.

But if they have such a horror of land-dwelling animals, they detest fish even more. It is true, however, that these are rare in the region because the birds of prey I just mentioned keep their numbers down. In thirty-two years I cannot recall seeing any except for a certain kind of eel three or four ells[11] in length and somewhat resembling a gleaming ebony-black porcupine.

11. An old unit of length, equivalent to 45 inches or 1.118 meters.

CHAPTER ELEVEN

On the Southern Land's
Useful Resources

Those who imagine that Europe is a self-contained region with no need of its neighbors are blind and ignorant. The new advantages arising from its trade with Asia and America over the past century are proof positive of this error. There can be no doubt that were it to enter into relations with the Australians it would become quite different to what it is now. I scarcely need mention their personal and moral virtues: these would provide an incomparable example and model to those among us who, even after thirty or forty years of mortifying the flesh, come nowhere near their perfection. I feel obliged to point out four great advantages that would immediately accrue from such contact.

Among the animals I have described, the Hums would be of inestimable benefit in relieving men of the worst agricultural burdens. But the Suefs would provide even greater satisfaction. They are such gentle creatures that they surpass even the most tractable of bullocks and are so easily kept that two pounds of grass feeds them for more than three days. Furthermore, they can fast for a whole day so that it is not necessary to break a journey of ten to twelve hours to feed them. Their stride is long and rapid, and in this time they can easily cover eighteen to twenty leagues. The profit they could be turned to by merchants and overlords[1] can easily be seen: travel and transport costs could be cut to a tenth. Two of these animals can carry the load of a six-horse wagon. The Australians, having no need of commerce, can be excused for making so little use of them; but Europeans should seek at all costs to acquire them because of the immense advantages to be gained.

But what surpasses anything Europe has known in the way of usefulness is the carnivorous bird species I have mentioned. These animals, so cruel in their wild state, can easily be tamed, becoming even more friendly and faithful than our dogs. They still had some in the seizain of Burd when I arrived that could carry a man more easily than a Spanish horse. You climb into the hollow between its wings, and the feathers of its backs form nice seats. You only have to pass a string through its beak to ride it anywhere, and they will easily go for twelve to sixteen hours at a stretch. After resting and feeding for two hours, they will do the same again. In this way one can cover in a day, without fear, difficulty, or danger, thirty or thirty-five leagues[2] as the crow flies, that is, without being bothered by obstacles such as rivers, forests, mountains, or unwelcome company. In a word, it is both an unparalleled convenience and an unspeakable pleasure.

Two reasons have caused the Australians to get rid of these creatures, neither of which would apply in Europe: firstly, they have an enormous appetite for carnal conjunction, which means that a male will often carry off his unfortunate passenger to an island where it has scented a female, and the Australian will end up being eaten by the birds. Secondly, it was found that the tame specimens attracted wild ones, resulting in the great disorders that they endured. These factors would not apply in the northern

1. *Seigneurs.*
2. About one hundred miles.

hemisphere because there would be only tame birds, which would bring only benefits. It is true that they are carnivorous, but they only eat men because they are enticed to do so, as I shall explain.

Such are the interesting features I have noticed about the animals of the Southern Land. As for its fruits, these surpass all imagination in beauty and delicacy, and the tables of princes and kings would be enriched by them. Apart from this, there are the miraculous properties of the Balf tree—the fortifying sleep it induces, in whatever measure is required, and the range of wounds its juice can rapidly heal—I am led to think that there is no disease in Europe for which it would not provide a sure remedy. I know, for example, that it was the only dressing used on my wounds when I arrived and that despite my numerous cuts, breaks, and bruises, I was completely healed within three days. Thus we could eliminate our innumerable drugs and medicines and cure ourselves at no cost, living free of the debilitating illnesses that kill most people in our part of the world.

I was subject to many infirmities during my years in Portugal, and the frightful trials I endured at sea must have weakened me further. But since I have been in this country and lived on its fruits, I must say that I have suffered no bodily ailment of any sort. And although my moral failings have caused me a lot of trouble and homesickness together with the strangeness of the customs I have had to practice often upset me, as soon as I eat a Balf fruit my resentment subsides, my heart becomes gay, and I find myself in a most agreeable mood. This comfort would be worth its weight in gold in the northern lands, where despair overtakes the majority of people and disappointments leads to depressions that are worse than death itself.

What could be more desirable than to live in luxury at no cost, without any need either to cook or have cooks nor any of the consequences they bring? What could be more delicious than to enjoy a cordial drink more nourishing and fortifying than any of the natural or artificial drinks of Europe, without effort or work but only pleasure? What a boon for our religious brethren to be able to live virtually without eating or drinking—without having to waste time and money on a host of preparations. Nothing more would be needed than three or four pieces of a fruit sweeter and more appetizing than our best and tastiest foods and a kind of nectar of a delicacy unknown in our lands, requiring no effort other than to pluck it from the hands of nature after some minimal cultivation.

Furthermore, because Europeans are so obsessed with novelties, they could produce all the experiments and inventions they wanted or needed, simply by mixing various concoctions of Balf juice and brine. Soft materials could be made harder than iron with no need of foundry or hammer, and what is hard made as soft and pliable as molten wax. In a word, no magician has ever approached the subtleties and curiosities produced from this mixture, and it is readily apparent that no one, however little experienced, would be unable to produce effects with it that we would rightly judge miraculous.[3]

I have many a time admired how profusely and yet playfully nature gives here what she is so begrudging of in our lands. All that we consider rare, charming, and valuable is so common to them that nothing is given less thought. What Europeans win only through long and difficult cultivation costs but a momentary exertion in that country. Nor can I help insisting on the abundance of fine rock crystal found there, which they dress and fit together so perfectly that one cannot see the joins, and which is so transparent that it would be invisible were it not for the streaks of color nature had placed in it.

I take it as proof that the country has been razed to its present flatness, that there exists in a seizain of Huff a Hab apparently

---

3. This paragraph and the preceding one were omitted in 1692, leaving only the soberest elements of Foigny's imaginary science.

made of a single block of stone; which could only have been possible by carving it out of the living rock. It is a prodigy of size and richness, even compared to their ordinary Habs; the patterns in the crystal are finer than usual and can be followed throughout the building's entire length without a break. But I was told that they had already proposed several times in their assemblies that it would be better to destroy it than to conserve it: firstly, because it aroused curiosity; secondly, because it was a distraction; and thirdly, because it was a local particularity. But I do not know what decision was reached. The European Christians who seek so assiduously to decorate and enrich their churches would find there everything they could wish for to that end.

The great difficulty, however, is to find the means of communicating with these people; and after studying this problem in the greatest possible depth, I can see only insurmountable difficulties. Because they desire nothing, there is no reason to believe that they could be won over by the lure of gain, payment, or pleasure.[4] Moreover, the inexplicable aversion they display and cultivate for our kind proves that they cannot relate to us except with repugnance. We are hated by them no less than we hate wolves and snakes, and they cannot hear of our nature without betraying their passion[5] for destroying us.

The things we take to the so-called New World, by which we gain access and favor among its inhabitants, seem to them only trivialities and children's toys, unworthy of a man's consideration. They regard our textiles in the same way that we would consider so many spider's webs, and they do not know what the words gold and silver mean. In a word, all that we hold to be precious is in their eyes ridiculous and worthy only of beasts.

---

4. Echoing the early frustrations experienced by mercantile interests seeking to exploit New World markets.

5. Again, a manifest contradiction of the earlier postulates of "universal brotherhood," of an absence of passions and so on.

But the final obstacle to every avenue of communication that I have considered is the sea. It is so shallow around their coasts that it would keep even a small boat five or six hundred yards out and a ship two or three leagues offshore, except for some channels that can only be known through long experience. Furthermore, they maintain a coast guard so effective that it is impossible to surprise them or even attack them, as we shall now see.

CHAPTER TWELVE

The Australians' Regular Wars

It is a universal rule in this world that one cannot gain without effort, nor keep one's gains without difficulty. The Australians, who would be content with their natural wealth, accordingly lack neither enemies who hate them nor wars in which they must defend themselves. The most common are of three kinds: against the Fundians, the sea monsters, and the wild carnivorous birds. The first and second of these oblige them to keep standing armies at the foot of the Juad Mountains and, especially, on the coasts where they station twenty thousand men over a distance of sixty leagues. The third class of adversary requires that they stay together at certain times and take other great and inconvenient precautions.

The choice of troops to man these garrisons is made without the slightest difficulty. Their system has been ordered since time immemorial in such a way that all military arrangements are made without a single word being uttered. About six million people are drawn in from the surrounding countryside to guard the access routes, deploying themselves in such a way that three hundred and thirty will gather within a distance of one league, and more than one hundred thousand over three hundred leagues.

110

Anyone noticing an enemy incursion raises the alarm in the form of a brilliant flame that makes a noise like a waterfall and can be heard two leagues away. Others then relay the signal, so that within twenty-four hours the entire continent will have been alerted. Half of the guards hasten to the spot where the alarm was first raised, so rapidly that within six hours three to four thousand are in position. When it is deemed that enough have arrived to deal with the threat, the original signal is canceled and reinforcements cease to arrive.

What is most amazing of all to see is how, without any leader, without orders, and without even speaking, they position themselves with such skill and precision that no army was ever better deployed. Those arriving first at the scene form the van and advance according to the perceived need. Each has reason alone for his guide, and they fall in with such perfect agreement that one would think they shared a single mind or that each was a master strategist and tactician in his own right.

I was involved in two Fundian invasions, the first about seventeen years after my arrival and the other just last year. In the first, the Fundians gathered, about one hundred thousand strong, and attempted to force a passage where it was least expected. They posted some thirty thousand troops in a spot only fifty paces from Australian territory, and these marched in under cover of darkness so that if a few careless ones had not made a noise, more than ten thousand would have got in before the alarm was raised. The latter was doubled in view of the extreme danger, calling on all seizains to come.

To begin with, the horde of Fundians found only three hundred Australians who, nevertheless, fought so stoutly that they held up the advance. But because they were already surrounded, they were all killed. And yet, selling their lives dearly and holding out for two hours, they gave time for the neighboring seizains to arrive so that as they succumbed another force of about fifteen hundred was forming. The Fundians, advancing over the bodies of the first victims, swarmed in more than sixty thousand strong, shouting "Ham! Ham!" (Victory!). The fifteen hundred confronted them squarely and solidly, but the Fundians easily surrounded them, and a bloody battle ensued.

On the following day a detachment of Fundians, their lust aroused, attacked the fifteen hundred from all sides to destroy them or at least prevent their escape. The Australians had by now amassed about twenty-five thousand men, including myself, and formed three units of which the smallest, numbering five or six thousand, tried to reach the passage where the Fundians had got in. On learning this, the Fundians posted twenty thousand men in ambush, and these savaged the Australians so violently for over five hours that they would have all been killed if a reinforcement of three thousand had not arrived. This prolonged the battle for a further five hours, with a carnage on both sides that words cannot describe. The other two groups fought with the same vigor and brought the Fundian advance to a standstill.

The butchery was such that the field became an ocean of blood through which the combatants waded knee-deep. The Fundians began to weaken when a further reinforcement of twenty thousand Australians arrived, who cut through them without difficulty and relieved us. Then ten thousand men went to the aid of the brothers at the passage, who were suffering greatly from the Fundian ambushers. Those of the enemy inside the country were attacked anew and, being exhausted, decided to flee. Finding the roads closed off, however, and death inevitable, they turned desperately on the twenty thousand Australians pursuing them and cut a patch through them when the Australians were too slow in killing them. Escaping into the countryside, they dispersed here and there. The fighting went on until the middle of the following night, as the Australians mopped up, finally leaving none of the fugitive Fundians alive. Then they marched to the passage, where Fundians were still vigorously defending themselves.

But when they saw these Australian reinforcements arrive, they broke off and tried to retreat.

At last the battle was over, and the alarms canceled. The Australians who had fought rested and refreshed themselves, while newcomers gathered up the dead brothers. More than nineteen thousand had died on the field, and the wounded numbered twelve thousand, among whom I include myself, with a broken arm and a thigh wound. The dead were identified, and it was found that only twenty-seven from the two nearest seizains had survived. Arrangements were made for the bodies to be returned to their apartments, and those of the Fundians were piled up at the place where they had burst in. There were more than ninety thousand of them spread over a league and a half.

Such was the first battle of the Australians against the Fundians that I can describe as an eye witness. I observed no other behavior on our side than to stand firm and resolute to the death. Those in front would parry the assailants' blows while those behind launched their own, so effectively that fifty Australians can confront a horde of ten thousand. They all carry a kind of small shield, as light and delicate as paper but so hard as to be almost impenetrable. Each man had his rations provided from his own apartment, and their system of transport is all the more efficient in that it is scarcely noticeable: the brothers bring the food to their Hab in the morning, and neighbors passing through carry in on to the next Hab, and so on, until it arrives at the place where the troops are engaged. If the distance is such that it would spoil, it is exchanged for fresh fruits along the way.

The second battle took place sixteen years later. The Fundians had taken possession of an island ten leagues offshore from a seizain in Puls. It was a large island, nine hours across,[1] and because it was very fertile, they had fortified themselves and multiplied there. The sweetness of its air and its abundant

---

1. 1692: eighteen leagues by fourteen leagues.

production had attracted ever more colonies to it, and they had even discovered a means of raiding the Australian coast.

Once the decision had been made to drive them out of the place, no general alarm was necessary. It was simply written up in the five hundred neighboring seizains, which dispatched four hundred men each and assembled an army of two hundred thousand. A kind of platform or raft was built, three hundred men wide and four hundred long; it carried one hundred and twenty thousand men in battle formation, who would travel in the water if the raft was unable to carry them. As well, they equipped six smaller vessels each carrying one hundred men with provisions for one week, plus four hundred other boats carrying the provisions of those on the platform, and a further two hundred to come and go according to the army's needs.

One-third of these six hundred support vessels were used to transport three siege engines. The first of these consisted of a kind of organ-cannon with one thousand barrels able to fire simultaneously; the second, of a mechanical stepladder; and the third, of a number of mechanical wheels geared so as to drive a spike through walls, the spike then opening into a hook so that the machine could be further turned and drag stones out of the wall, causing it to collapse.

I was on the platform as this prodigious army trundled into action against the Fundians, who had been courageously preparing themselves for three months. It was the first time that the Australians had ever gone out to attack the Fundians; the latter had not believed them capable of leaving their country or even of defending themselves outside it. The Fundians had stocked themselves with provisions and secured stout defenses of double ditches and ramparts around the island. They were three hundred thousand in number, not counting a like number of women and girls, and were resolved either to win or to die.

The Australians, on arriving within range of the Fundian catapults, stopped to deliberate on the best means of penetration.

After serious consideration, it was decided to dispatch twenty thousand men from the platform to surround the island during the night. These would provoke the Fundians while another ten thousand would get ashore with the wall-boring machine. This was carried out so effectively that the Fundians did not have time to take action or even to realize what was happening. The ten thousand went straight to work on the first wall, and as soon as it was pierced, two thousand men swam through it and put the engine to the second wall. As it was being pierced, the Fundian guards heard the noise and did what they could under the circumstances. But the night was exceptionally dark and the Australians swam the two bodies of water with as much ease as we would walk, thus escaping detection.

More than twenty-five thousand of them got into the ditches, and then kept absolutely silent while the Fundians blocked up the two holes. Elsewhere, meanwhile, Australians were attacking vigorously in ten or twelve places; several even climbed the walls and sacrificed themselves to the defenders, who thus learned— although too late—that their ancient enemies were even more powerful on attack than in defense. The Australians in the ditches, having rested briefly, began to scale the second wall, and five hundred of them landed on the other side and regrouped to meet the defenders' onslaught and help those coming behind them. After one hour, twenty thousand of them had assembled inside the walls despite all the efforts of the Fundians. When their king learned of this, he took command of a reserve corps of sixty thousand men and came to meet the invaders.

The Australians raised a battle cry to inform the others that they were inside the walls, and then began a battle so ferocious on both sides that the dead and wounded fell like the fruits of a strongly shaken tree. The other brothers, realizing the courage and determination of their opponents, climbed the walls every- where and in spite of the Fundians' resistance, which was as spirited as can be imagined, more than fifty thousand of them got over. Some of these then went to the aid of the first five thousand while the others took possession of the rest of the island. Just as day broke they relieved their brothers, who were about to succumb. They redoubled their battle cries and, having taken over a part of the walls, allowed the vessels to come alongside. Using the ladder-engine, more than twenty thousand men poured in within two hours.

The Fundians regrouped into a formation of one hundred thousand men for a final all-out effort, and attacked the fifty thousand Australians with such virulence that these, although resisting strongly, would have been lost if another body of Australians, having dragged down more than two hundred fathoms[2] of wall, had not come to their aid. This was a detachment of sixty thousand from the platform, fresh and fighting fit; they attacked the Fundians in the rear and made such carnage that barely two thousand of the enemy survived to flee into a small fortress nearby.

Finally, by 3:00 P.M. the island was won. Before the mopping up of the remaining eighteen forts began, all the coasts and vessels were secured to prevent any Fundians from escaping. This took two days, and a further two were spent gathering up the dead brothers' bodies, which numbered over forty-two thousand. They were loaded onto the platform and taken back to Australia[3] for burial. The Fundian dead too were counted, at one hundred and twenty thousand, and a reinforcement of fifty thousand joined the Australians. With these tasks completed, a thorough combing of the towns and villages was carried out. Five were immediately taken, in which forty thousand of the enemy were butchered with incredible ferocity.

It is hard to imagine how much I desired the females I encountered at this time, nor could I see them without feeling a

2. Four hundred yards.
3. *{Sic}*: this is the first known use of the name.

compassion that was noticed by a number of Australians. I went into a house that seemed more substantial than the others and found a venerable matron with two daughters of twenty-five or twenty-six, who flung themselves at my feet. I was overcome with love, and the charms of their faces and naked breasts made me lose all sense and reason. I raised them up and kissed them, and when I seized one of them she offered no resistance. But I had barely begun when two Australians burst in and caught me in the act. I could see from their expressions that I was done for, but they were content to massacre the ladies in front of me. After that I knew neither what would become of me nor what I should do, and I could no longer face an Australian without shame. When they approached I could only hang my head. I returned to the mainland in one of the ships, pretending to be wounded, and was, indeed, so stricken with grief and sorrow that I could scarcely live with myself.

When the flat lands and towns had been sacked, the strongholds were attacked. Three were surrounded at a time. Their method of laying siege was to induce an earthquake or subsidence; thirty thousand were engaged to dig around the place while the rest protected them. This ditch reached the walls within three days. In spite of the Fundians' countermeasures and their various attempts to escape, both underground and above, all the walls were torn down and the towns leveled, to the great consternation of the inhabitants. Then a general assault was launched, and all the ardor of the defending Fundians was unable to prevent the three strongholds from being taken within three or four days. The slaughter that followed would make even the most hardened tremble, if it could be described. A father, mother, and five or six children would be cut down together, and rivers of blood ran through the streets. No one, of any age or condition, was spared.[4]

4. These details and the crucially important encounter with the Fundian girl were omitted in the 1692 version. Note that *Fund* signifies in Australian "dry/earth/black/unpleasant."

The other forts saw the same fate in store for them and evacuated the night or day before it was their turn. More than fifty thousand people of all sorts could be seen on the beaches, some leaping into the water, others throwing themselves on the mercy of their enemies; others again awaiting, with hands raised to heaven, the death they could see was inevitable.

In this way that fine island was turned into a desert, and when a final count was made of the dead it was found that a total of 398,956 were piled up on the seashore for the carnivorous birds to dispose of. In addition to the Australian dead mentioned in the account of the assault, a further eighteen thousand were found and taken to the mainland, and the wounded from both attacks totaled more than thirty thousand.

It is noteworthy that the Australians observed the assemblies of the Hab and Heb outside of their country as well as in it, with the sole difference that their times were not so strictly regulated. Thus as soon as the island was securely in their possession they assembled to praise God and deliberate over the events that had taken place. The main problems were how to deal with me, and how to complete the destruction of the island. I was accused of five crimes each punishable by death, and when I had been heard was sent back to my seizain. As for the island, it was decided to raze it, using two parties of fifty thousand men. That prodigious mass of earth was entirely destroyed and covered with water within ten of their months, an undertaking not only impossible in ten years for Europeans, but even inconceivable and horrifying. This, then, is what I have seen of the Australians' wars with the Fundians.

Their second type of enemy is the sea monster, which means, from what I can gather, Europeans. They are distinguished from Fundians only by the fact that the Australians know where the latter come from, whereas of the former they can speak only in confused terms. They know they are all half-men, but because their ways of speaking and dressing are all different and they cannot distinguish where they come from, they call them collectively sea monsters, unknown monsters, or marine half-men.

Before my good friend retired from the world, he discussed our respective countries a number of times with me, and although he did not believe much of what I told him, I knew that he was greatly interested. He described similar people he had seen, whose vessels he had admired and some fragments of which he showed me. He added that he had always hoped to learn something about these half-men, and that what I said fitted in with his own reasonings.

He gave me to understand that he had seen some who were much braver than others. Once, he said, the Australians had dealt with some powerful warriors who arrived in seven ships and resisted defeat for three days. I have seen these ships, and more than five hundred others preserved around the coasts from time immemorial because it is their custom not to destroy such trophies. Not six months before my arrival another fleet had come to grief, and there were even still twenty-eight corpses to be seen hanging from the vessels' spars. I could easily make out that it was a fleet, or two fleets combined, of French and Portuguese ships. The French flagship bore the motto "United" and the French coat of arms; the Portuguese one had the arms of the House of Portugal opposite those of Braganza.

My old sage, who had witnessed the battle fought on that occasion, assured me that apart from my fight with the birds, he had never seen anything like it. The skill of their master pilot had enabled them to penetrate half an hour inside the coast, up an inlet where, the water becoming less than six inches deep, he had put one thousand men ashore to reconnoiter the country. They struck with extraordinary force, easily overcoming the coast guard. The alarm was hastily raised and doubled because the intruders were penetrating violently into the first quarter of a seizain of the land of Puls. Before the Europeans had managed to seize the plunder they sought, more than eight thousand Australians had gathered on the shore. The ships' cannon thundered loudly but were out of range. The thousand raiders were surrounded while sacking a house, in which they defended themselves for a while. But they eventually succumbed to superior numbers, and none lived to tell the tale.

Then the Australians made a long detour to block the channel by which the ships had entered, being able to seal the passages so effectively with heaps of earth that no escape was possible. Having done that, they prepared to board. The carnage that then ensued was such that it even surprised these people who consider themselves incapable of fear. Of the eight thousand who advanced, six thousand were cut down by a combined volley from the ships; the old man declared that he had never seen anything like it nor believed it possible.

But as reinforcements poured in from everywhere to replace those lost, a second attack was mounted consisting of twelve thousand men. These were again treated very savagely but did not sustain as many losses as the first lot. They courageously, or rather desperately, battled their way to the ships. As they climbed them they were shot at point-blank range by the armed Europeans, and in that frightful carnage more than seven thousand died. This attack lasted for over two hours before a further twenty thousand Australians arrived and, finding the enemy dropping from fatigue and (as far as I can gather) at the end of their ammunition, overcame them. There were three thousand soldiers in the ships and as many sailors, all killed and hung in the rigging.[5] The Australian dead totaled 10,615 with 6,000 wounded.

As mentioned, the regular fights they have with the birds cause even worse problems because these invaders come and go

---

5. The number of Europeans seems excessive in relation to real activities in the region at the time and further complicates the numerological inflation in which the austral experience culminates.

in the air, and there is no way either of preventing them or of destroying them. They are encountered in three ways: in the first two they attack the Australians, whereas in the third the fight is taken to them. The first is the surprise attack. The birds sometimes hide in trees or else soar high into the air, out of sight, before swooping down on their prey. The little pet birds I mentioned can smell them from a long way off and give a sad and urgent cry, or even a few pecks, to warn the Australians. Even so, these enemies are so subtle and clever that it is hard to escape them.

I was walking to the Hab one day with my philosopher and three others, when we were suddenly attacked. Armed in the usual manner with halberd, helmet, and shield, we were barely halfway there when our little birds cried out with extraordinary shrillness, flitting about in a terrified manner to warn us of the danger. Just then six of the beasts attacked us furiously. We pressed close together, covering ourselves with our armor and parrying the blows. One of them seized the shaft of my halberd and tore it right out of my hand, while the others gave my companions such trouble that they could barely defend themselves. The moment I turned to help them I was hoisted off the ground and would certainly have been lost if the five brothers had not rushed to my aid and freed me. The deadliness of these birds is such that one can rarely strike them, if among a small group of companions, without being carried off. The experienced make no attempt to attack them under such circumstances, and in any case it would be a wasted effort because their bellies are as impenetrable as a shield.

As well as making these surprise attacks, they sometimes appear in flocks of four or five thousand with a clamor that would terrify even the bravest. Not surprisingly, they use special tactics, forming themselves into a sort of military unit. They wander anywhere where there is food, leaving their homelands for two to three months of the year. During this time the Australians keep indoors and never go out alone. The alarm is raised when they appear, and the neighboring seizains assemble four or five thousand men in defense. Their military organization is then even more precise than for the wars against the Fundians. They press close together in a square formation, presenting a front on all sides and armed with the "organs," or cannon, I mentioned earlier, as well as carrying their halberds and several cutlasses.

The moment they see the Australians coming out against them, the birds split up so cunningly that it appears to be a deliberate stratagem: they position themselves on each side, then soar out of sight and reform into a single unit before swooping down on their victims. The latter, in spite of their arms and defensive ploys, always lose a few of their number. We lost six in my first such encounter, eight in the second, and three in the last, and in all these fights we killed only seven birds. It is impossible to describe their bold advances, the violence of their blows, or the speed with which they maneuver.

One such incident during my last encounter with them deserves retelling. An Urg seized my companion's halberd; another grasped hold of him at the same time. I tried to defend him with my halberd, but a third Urg took it from me. Another companion held on to the brother being carried off, but the bird hoisted them both up; yet another brother held on, but an Urg threw me against him. When it began to carry him off I held on to him; and we would all four have been lost had we not managed to kill one of the birds. The first brother taken had been strangled to death by the time we freed him.

These fights go on until nightfall, and the menace is such that one cannot even breathe easily, let alone take one's eyes off the enemy. To let one's attention wander, however briefly, is to be struck down or carried off. I do not know whether it is hunger, lust, or a kind of rage that affects them in this way, but they behave like desperados, and if they were like this all the time, the country would soon be uninhabitable. It is known that when the sea has been stormy for five or six days continuously, they are provoked to behave in this way: perhaps because they cannot catch the fish they normally live on, or because the disturbance of the weather also affects their brains.

I mentioned that the Australians have made, and still make every year, a great effort to rid themselves of these horrible enemies. They have razed three large islands some two leagues across in the last thirty years and are currently engaged in destroying another one six hours from the coast. In these cases they go on the attack. Their strategy is to choose the right moment and invade the island with an army of thirty thousand men, rotating in monthly shifts of four thousand each. The most convenient time for this is the Capricorn solstice because the birds then display some sort of timidity that makes them retreat without a fight after circling their island three or four times.

Once the Australians are established there, the noisy machines they bring keep the birds away, and they also light fires everywhere, which further frightens the Urgs. Thus they can set to work relatively peacefully to demolish the island until the March equinox when the birds begin their rut and again become menacing, although not seriously so until the sun enters Taurus. Then they return in hordes to attack the Australians with such ferocity that, whatever precautions are taken, the latter cannot avoid losing men and goods. The heat of this terrible conflict lasts for ten hours at a stretch, with no let-up for a month. After this the birds' ardor dies down until the month of October, when it again waxes as fierce as in April.

CHAPTER THIRTEEN

Sadeur's Return as Far as Madagascar

I write the following at the island of Madagascar and am beginning to feel confident that my story may eventually reach and edify my compatriots. It will be clear from all I have related that differences of nature and upbringing made me incompatible with the Australians. It is equally certain that I owed my survival among them solely to my desperate behavior on arrival and to the continual effort I made to conform to their ways—especially after the warnings of the old man who was protecting me.

However, because nature cannot be overcome I still could not help constantly revealing myself for what I was. While he lived, my old philosopher kept haranguing the brothers to keep them from destroying me, representing my fight with the birds as an unheard-of prodigy that should alone suffice to keep me in favor, whatever my other faults. He said that because they had let me live, knowing that I was unnatural, they could not justifiably take away that right because of faults arising from my nature. He added that as a foreigner, after all, I could not be condemned without warning nor without their being certain that I was incorrigible. When he decided to retire from life, he redoubled his pleas and arguments on my behalf. He named me his lieutenant and delivered a truly paternal oration about me, so that the brothers again consented to tolerate me. Thus I was accepted until the Fundian war I have mentioned, when my fate was finally sealed.

I was accused then on five main counts: firstly, that I had not fought, as was proven by the fact that I had not taken any Fundian ears; secondly, that I had shown distress at the destruction of the enemy; thirdly, that I had conjoined myself carnally with a Fundian woman; fourthly, that I had eaten Fundian food; and fifthly, that I had asked seditious questions. To understand all these charges it is necessary to know, firstly, that the Australian custom is to cut off their victims' ears as trophies of war and make belts out of them. Whoever collects the most is considered the most heroic, and in that invasion, some had taken as many as two hundred. Far from having killed, however, I had shown much regret at the bloody slaughter of those unfortunate victims. My carnal lusts I mentioned in chapter 4, and as for conjunction with a Fundian woman, this is considered a crime of the same order as bestiality in Europe. As soon as my deed became known, they refused to look at me or speak to me. They also detest Fundian cuisine and consider it beneath their dignity to eat such food. Another of my crimes was to have suggested keeping at least a few Fundian women as slaves—that I would prefer such booty to any other kind.

When these charges had been heard, it was suggested in a hostile manner that I be invited to take the Balf, which I willingly undertook to do. A long silence ensued as they waited for me to step up to the table and take the fruit in the usual way. Then I spoke up, saying that I felt so obliged to the brothers that I did not wish to leave them without passing on a great secret I knew that would enable them to dispose easily of the Urgs. This was greeted by further silence. I added that I was indeed guilty of what I had been accused of, but that because the origin of these crimes was in my own nature, which was known to be a Fundian one, and because they had tolerated me as a Fundian, reason dictated that they should also tolerate these faults arising from my nature.

It was true, I said, that I was unable to kill my own people; it was true that I had shown compassion for others. But had I not done so I would be an unnatural monster, and the Australians' clairvoyant reason would then be right in condemning me as cruel. If it came to pass that an Australian fell among the Fundians, I asked, would it not be excusable—supposing that he did not kill himself immediately as he would be expected to— if he showed humanity and favor toward his brothers?[1] I protested that I was not seeking to prolong my life, that I was delighted to retire from it, but that I could leave a good memory of the poor stranger who had come among them if granted a brief stay of execution.

They left the Hab in the usual way without making any reply, and I immediately set about inventing a means of escape. I had in mind particularly the circumstances of my arrival, and thought it easy rather than dangerous to risk the sea again. I thought constantly about my plank and told myself that Providence had not abandoned me, that what had brought me there could take me back in similar fashion. I prayed for some enlightenment about a means of escape. It seemed that if I could only get out of the Australians' sight, it would be possible. Finally, after much thought and a multitude of fruitless schemes, I devised and executed the following plan.

I made a rope from the bark of the Schueb tree and rubbed it with Balf juice mixed with a drop of seawater to make it as hard as iron and then with another juice to make it flexible. This I formed into a trap and set it in a tree where Urgs were in the habit

1. Note the argument from cultural relativity, turning the postulate of universal brotherhood against itself; and compare also the circumstances of Foigny's own trial in Geneva, following the book's publication.

of perching. I came and went impatiently, hoping for the desired effect, until my little birds warned me to withdraw, and two Urgs came down to perch, one of them putting its foot into the trap.

The brothers watching this experiment hastened to kill the bird, but I begged them to wait and see the full fruits of their trust. The captive beast would not let me approach for two days, but finally, seeing that it had no chance of escaping and forced by hunger, it allowed me to come to it with food. Because I was the only one who fed it, it soon got to know me and would let me handle it, climb onto its back, and even examine its claws and open its beak. Eventually I felt no fear in its company and said to myself as I handled it, "Could it be that, having arrived in this land through the cruelty of these beasts, I shall leave it by means of their friendship?" I was hopeful of this, and became more so as the bird's friendship grew.

My behavior was questioned in the Hab, but I replied that I was already beginning to regard myself as ceasing to exist: that it was the custom of my people to withdraw from the world at the approach of death; that my mind was no longer the same, knowing that I would soon cease to be; and that I was devoting my remaining moments to a glorious deed that they would honor much more than my previous one.[2] These reasons satisfied the Assembly, which decreed that I be left alone to do whatever I wished—that no further thought be given to me because I was already to be considered one of the dead. They even ordained my lieutenant and ceased to regard me as anything but a dying man. This pleased me immensely, and I regarded it as the means of my deliverance.

I spent nearly all my time with my bird, showering it with affection. One day I noticed it had difficulty standing up because the rope tethering it had been too tight and had cut into its foot. The wound was deep and serious, and I went to great lengths to

2. Again, a parody of Christ's Resurrection is evident.

relieve it. I dressed and bandaged it properly for a week until it was perfectly healed, and the creature's gratitude was then such that it would not let me out of its sight, and I too was happy in its company. I let it go free, and instead of flying away it persisted in following me everywhere.

Then I tried an experiment to see whether it could carry me in the air and found that it would do so with admirable ease and pleasure. I made myself a girdle of leaves rubbed with Balf juice to make it waterproof and formed this into a sort of hollow sash into which I put a number of the best Balf fruits I could find and some bottles of its juice. I also made a small case and filled it with fruit for my bird, and having secured this on its back, I prepared to leave that night. It was the 15th of the Capricorn solstice, in the thirty-fifth year after my arrival there and the fifty-seventh of my life. The memory of all the frightful dangers I had been exposed to on my voyage there, far from disturbing me, only increased my hopes.

In order for my mount to take off more easily, I got it to climb into a tree, from which, seated in the crook of its wings, I set out on my great return voyage full of hope and confidence. At first my fear of being seen by the coast guard made me steer the bird high into the air, but the coldness of the upper regions soon brought me down again. We traveled for about six hours and then, whether because its old wound was troubling it or because its long rest had made it put on weight, the bird began to tire. I brought it down to let it sit on the sea, getting off and letting my girdle support me in the water. The animal, however, fearing that I would drown or that I was leaving it, became pitifully agitated, huddling close to comfort me. I laid my head on is feathers after giving it some fruits from the food hamper, and fell asleep.

Waking up to a fine day, I gave the bird some more fruits and had some myself, before remounting ready to set off. But the bird was unable to take off with my weight pressing it into the water, whatever it or I did, which was very disturbing. After a while I remembered that the creatures swam strongly and got it to tow me by its tail. It did this so effectively that I eventually sighted an island far away on the horizon. With night approaching I decided to stop there, and we ate together.

After this the bird, whether from homesickness, the changing atmosphere, or because it was troubled to see me in this state, indicated that it did not wish to go any further, signaling with its beak that we should return. Seeing that I did not agree, it began to get angry and only calmed down when I pretended to make preparations for returning. Finally, with nightfall it fell into a deep sleep. Deciding that God had shown me a sign that from now on I should depend only on his Providence (as previously), I gently untied the bag from the bird's back and moved away, intending to leave it although with great regret.

"Lord," I prayed from the bottom of my soul, "it is your will that I should depend on you and be entirely guided by your Providence. I accept and embrace your will as my only guide. I am ashamed and embarrassed that you show so much concern for such a worthless subject. You do too much, Father of Compassion, far too much for such a miserable wretch. I should have liked to return and announce your wonders and miracles to the people you have chosen above all others to know you, bless you, and enjoy your glory, but for fear of asking too much, I abandon myself and submit to your pleasure. At least I shall die knowing that I was not my own killer against your will." These were approximately my words, washed with tears.

Knowing that my girdle and sash would keep me afloat, and my hamper support me as I swam, I set off for good from the bird and with the help of a good southerly breeze arrived at the island I had seen. I got ashore without difficulty and ate some fruits, with inner joy at the knowledge of God's benevolence towards me. Then sleep overtook me, and I slept for about six hours. I awoke resolved to press on, heading northeast rather than the north for fear of remaining within the ocean that separates the

Old World from the New. But as I entered the water I heard the sound of a carnivorous bird in flight, and my stomach turned over with a sensation of impending doom. But this turned to joy when I realized that my pet bird had come to find me. It flung itself at my feet with such caresses and expressions of grief at my abandoning it that I took pity on it. Realizing that it was exhausted and had made a long flight to find me, I stayed a day and a night at the island to rest and feed it.

After an hour and a half, however, ten creatures the size and almost the color of our wolves approached. The bird noticed them first and fell on them with such speed and violence that it put them to flight. It caught one, raised it in the air, and flung it at another, killing it. As the others retreated, it flew after them and caught a third, which it partly ate before returning to me. When night fell, it became very restless except when I was beside it so that I could not move away without waking it up. I slept with it for six or seven hours.

When it awoke, it devoured one of the animals it had killed. I ate some fruits, and then without delay led it to a rock and climbed onto its back as before and took off. It proceeded at a very brisk pace, and we had already covered a long distance when two other birds of its size encountered us and attacked violently with their beaks and claws. It was inevitable that my poor bird must succumb, being both laden and outnumbered. I had already received several blows and was bleeding all over when I decided to jump into the water. There I watched the fight for a while; my bird simply waited with its beak and claws ready to take advantage of any opportunity they gave it. Then a fog hid them from sight, to my regret, and I could not help falling into a profound melancholy, which made me think back over the misery that my sins had led me into.

The Southern Land came to mind with all its advantages, and even the island I had just left seemed extremely desirable. I could have stayed on there, I told myself, without danger or fear for the rest of my days with my bird for a bodyguard. By contrast, it seemed that I was unable to make any progress in my present plans without abusing God's goodness and tempting him; I only fell back into the same clutches of death that I so feared. My sin seemed even greater in that I could have justified staying on where I had been on the grounds of the need to observe the laws of the land, whereas now I was led only by despair.

The worst of my misfortune was that I did not know which way to turn, given that I could not see thirty paces away and that, because I had nothing for buoyancy, I could move only with difficulty. While mulling over these problems, I heard the loud noise of a sailing vessel. I was wondering whether I should shout out when some sailors noticed me and fired a number of shots, wounding me in various places. When the ship had come close enough for them to see that I resembled a man, they showed compassion and got me aboard. They wore a kind of garment that I had seen on two vessels wrecked on the Australian coasts, that covered the chest and thighs but left the parts we call shameful exposed. They were kind enough to dress my wounds, feed me, and give me a fortifying drink. After examining me, they concluded, in spite of my protestations to the contrary, that I was an Australian. I presented them with some of my fruits, which although by now overripe, greatly impressed them, and they gave me no rest until my bandolier was empty. My little bottles of juice charmed them to such a degree that they could not stop swigging on them and singing the praises of the land that had produced them.

After a week we arrived at their island, where word spread immediately that they had captured an Australian. Huge crowds gathered to see me, two or three thousand a day. After deliberating over what to do with me, they decided to do as the Australians do to their visitors. Because this was the first time they had caught an Australian, a public feast was organized for the day of my sacrifice. I no longer possessed anything but my girdle, one foot wide and six inches thick. They tried to get it off me but, finding it too close-fitting and fearing to break it, decided to wait until after my execution so as to remove it whole.

The people gathering for this occasion were so numerous that they filled a large square, in the middle of which I was tied onto a sort of scaffold thirty feet high. A clamor of excitement and applause went up as four of their leaders came with spikes and pricked me.[3] Having collected some of my blood in small goblets, they turned to the crowd and with certain gestures and words joyfully drank my blood to the last drop. Then two of the strongest hoisted me onto their shoulders, one thigh each, and two young men walked in front of them with four spikes and the four goblets used previously. My impression was that they planned to let me be pricked and my blood drunk by others and then my flesh be eaten for as long as it lasted.

But they were interrupted by a volley of cannon fired at the port where the garrison raised the alarm. The entire crowd vanished as if into thin air, and those carrying me dropped and abandoned me. I cannot describe my feelings at that moment, because I was in a sort of delirium that prevented me from either seeing or hearing. It reduced me to a despair in which dark thoughts crowded into my mind, and I was no longer myself. But this unexpected turn of events caused me to breathe again and to revive somewhat. Once alone, I tried to get up but was so weak that I could not stay on my feet. However, my great passion to survive gave me the strength to drag myself on all fours, without knowing where to except that it was the direction opposite to where my enemies had gone. I rubbed my girdle with some saliva in a certain place, making a hole through which I drew out three fruits and two bottles of juice. These, although past their best,

---

3. An explicit reference to the Crucifixion. It is clear too that many elements of this story anticipate both Defoe's *Robinson Crusoe* (1719) and Swift's *Gulliver's Travels* (1726).

still had enough strength left to sustain me and give me the courage to go on.

I had scarcely gone one hundred paces when I saw some men dressed in European fashion running toward me. I threw myself at their knees and begged them in Latin, my hands clasped in prayer, to have pity on their poor brother whom many misfortunes had kept in these parts for years, and who would have met with a horrible end but for their timely arrival. Two of the dozen men heard me and, recognizing what I was,[4] took me back to their vessels. I learned that they were three French ships out of Madagascar, seeking booty and fortune. They found none in this island, where the people had taken refuge in an inaccessible cave, and after seizing a few things they returned to their vessels.[5]

The commander, a well-to-do and respectable man, treated me very decently and, because I was a European, gave me some clothes and had me eat at his table. My first conversation with him lasted three hours, during which time I recounted the story of my birth and upbringing, my shipwrecks, and my arrival in the Southern Land. He listened sympathetically and was astonished that anyone could endure so much and survive so many dangers. I noticed that he relayed to the company in French what I told him in Latin, and that they all shrugged their shoulders and wondered how I could still be alive.

Then he had the discretion to let me eat in peace, but because I had grown unaccustomed to European foods and cookery, I found I had little taste for it and digested it with difficulty. Instead I ate the last of my fruits, now beginning to lose their taste, and finished my bottles of juice that were beginning to dry up. I offered one to the captain, who tried it and exclaimed that

4. Presumably, they took him to be a missionary.

5. The whole episode, from Sadeur's rescue by the islanders up to this point, was omitted in 1692; his first rescue then becomes that by the French, which is only briefly mentioned.

he had never before drunk anything so delicious. He asked me for another and gave it to the master pilot; then he wanted a third, a fourth, and so on, until my girdle was empty. There was none who did not admire the color and delicacy of those fruits, and they could not believe that they were natural.

When the meal was over, I had to repeat my story, going into as much detail as I could about the Southern Land, its inhabitants, and their customs. I gave the captain so many details that he declared several times his desire to go and enjoy the same experience, even at the risk of his life and worldly goods. He also drew a number of conclusions from my description of the Southern Land, considering it inevitable, from what I had said of the difficulties of entering it, that his companions would perish there.

We arrived after a week of variable weather at the port of Tonbolo, which is by no means austral, being in the southwest of Madagascar. The captain's benevolence continued, and I left him only because the governor of Tonbolo sought my company. I learned that the place where I had been rescued was one of the islands called austral,[6] and that the locals called it Ausicamt or Oscamt. The French were extremely desirous of occupying it as a more convenient and less dangerous stopover than the Cape of Good Hope. But this was an undertaking requiring more time and men than the governor could then afford.

---

6. It is unclear whether this refers to a cultural or a geographical configuration. In Renaissance times the region to the southeast of Asia was referred to in general as the "Austral Indies." Tonbolo may, notes Ronzeaud (1990, 49, 230), be the Tonobaia shown on a 1651 map of Madagascar, which also shows a port of Amanbal in the south of the island (possibly the Annanbolo approached on the outward journey [see chap. 3]).

CHAPTER FOURTEEN

Sadeur's Stay on the Island of Madagascar

Tonbolo, where we arrived, is a port attached to a small town inhabited by five or six thousand households. Of these the majority are French, some are Portuguese, others English, and a very few Dutch. There are still some natives there who are proving difficult to civilize. It lies under the Tropic of Capricorn on the 65th meridian in Ptolemy's system. The land is not only poor, but even unhealthy, as far as I could judge. The only food seen there is imported from elsewhere, and the natives who have not been subjugated are nomadic. They live without forethought and are ruled only by their passions.

After several discussions with the governor, I asked him for some men to make an expedition up the river they call Sildem to explore the interior. What aroused this desire in me was the river's majesty as it flowed out to the sea, which seemed to promise a hinterland worthy of exploration. He told me that he had had the same idea but that the inhabitants were so savage that they spared no one. They had captured two of his soldiers about three months previously and, according to a native from the region, had strung them up by their feet in trees five or six paces apart and swung them against each other until they died. A horde of children had crowded around to gather their blood and brains, and the corpses had been cut down and eaten on the spot as dogs would devour carrion. To avenge the death of these two he had chosen thirty horsemen and descended on the group responsible, massacring them violently before they realized what was happening. But as he was withdrawing he had been surrounded by a great number of these savages, who although small and thickset were more than terrifying with their horrible shouts and blows. He had made a great effort to force a way through them or, at least, to sell his life dearly and killed a large number before escaping with the loss of fifteen horsemen.[1]

This is what I have learned from the French colonists about the natives of the country, and I have no doubt that they are descended from the Kaffirs of Africa. Their physical makeup, their customs, and way of life are incontestable proof of this.

I was constantly amazed that such a large island, so well situated, could remain so little inhabited and cultivated. The more I thought about it, the more puzzled I was and the less able to explain it. But one day a French ship brought to the port a well-made boat, more round than oval in section and with bird beaks at its prow and stern. They had seized it as it made its way to an austral island, manned only by an old chief and his six rowers or servants. This man was almost of Australian build although his forehead and chin were more square than long, his hair black, his skin brown, and his body naked except for his private parts, which were covered by a delicate girdle one foot wide. As soon as I saw him, I was seized with compassion and a great desire to talk to him. The governor made no difficulty about my seeing him, hoping that I might find out some useful information about the region although he did not really expect me to.

I approached the old man, giving him to understand by signs that I was reduced to the same plight as he, which gave him some

1. The 1692 edition omits the Frenchman's retaliation.

consolation. After three or four sessions, I had worked out a means of communicating with him as follows: we agreed by signs to use certain words to express our thoughts, and I formulated more than two hundred of these in a night, which he readily understood.[2] Within two months, we had put together a language quite adequate to our needs. I told him all that had befallen me, of my stay in the Southern Land and my return from it.

When he was sufficiently persuaded of my sincerity, he became quite open about his own country. He gave me to understand that it comprised the middle part of an island, that it had a healthy climate, fertile soil, and highly civilized population. He explained that they were separated from wild and barbarous neighbors by two high mountain ramparts to the east and west, the latter called Canor and the former, Harnor. As for the two coasts to the north and south, these were protected by so many sandbanks that they could be approached only with many years' experience. Their country was about one hundred leagues in diameter and its government aristocratic or oligarchic: six governors were chosen every three years, one each from the parts facing the coasts and mountains and two from the interior. These governors each administered their regions and were obeyed on pain of an ignominious death.

From what I could gather, they cultivated the land in almost European fashion, sowing and harvesting although with different crops. The animals they used to break the ground were the size of our elephants. They suffered greatly from giant birds that they called Ruch,[3] and which could carry off an Orbus, a beast the size of our bullocks. He said, although with some

2. A reference to convention or social-contract theories of the origin of language, prevalent at the time (cf. chap. 9, n. 1).

3. See introduction, n. 31; chap. 10, n. 8. Note also that the frigate bird is a common motif in Melanesian and Polynesian art, that bird beaks decorate canoes, and that the canoe in general symbolizes the community (as does the "ship of state" in European cultures). Again, the ensuing story

disdain, that his people loved their liberty more than life,[4] that he was one of the governors he had spoken of, and that the misfortune of his capture had arisen from an unseasonal storm that had blown up as he went to investigate some sandbanks that had grown large enough to support a community. This had driven him far from his homeland, and when a weakness or curiosity induced him to delay his death, he had fallen into the hands of the foreigners. He added, however, that meeting me had been a great consolation to him so that he did not regret surviving this misfortune.

Eventually, after four months of very close relations with him, I was faced with a dilemma. Two Italian vessels returning from a visit to the Mogul arrived, due to continue on in two days to Livorno. I was loathe to tear myself away from such a close relationship, and yet for fear of wasting this opportunity, I made known my intention to sail with them. The old man asked the governor for permission to accompany me but this was refused because the governor was hoping to make a large ransom out of his capture.

I went to the old man to take my leave, but he replied coldly that he would be the first to leave and asked me to ensure that his body would be cast into the sea, it being a property of their corpses always to return to their homeland. He threw himself at my feet and declared his great regard for me, and then shouted five or six times in his own language. Two of his servants came and wrung his neck before knocking their own heads together so hard that they fell down dead. The other four, although elsewhere at the time, did the same. They were all found dead at once, to the great astonishment of the governor and his officials.

of the islanders' bodies returning to their homeland may parody a similar legend among the Polynesians, of their lost homeland Hawaiki and the soul's voyage to it at death.

4. This detail was omitted in 1692.

I told the story of the old man's death and the plea he had made before dying. The governor, to test this proposition, had the seven bodies thrown into the sea. It was calm and without current at the time, but everyone witnessed with amazement how they arranged themselves in such a way that the chief's body proceeded eastwards at walking speed, the other six following at a spacing of two paces. After they had gone about one league, the governor ordered that they be retrieved and separated widely from each other. The chief's[5] body was cast to the northwest and the others to the southwest, a good league away. But the former resumed its original course while the others waited until it came within a certain distance, and then it again drew them into line behind it as before.

More than one hundred of us witnessed this spectacle, each interpreting it differently. I said that, without a doubt, these bodies were like magnets, the strongest of which exerted the greatest attraction—that the chief's was clearly the most magnetic because of his superior nutrition and parentage. I added that what drew their bodies eastward was their homeland, acting as a magnetic pole in relation to everything that came from it, that such was certainly the explanation of this apparently miraculous attraction. Three leagues away a cape jutted more than two miles out into the sea, and three boats the governor sent to follow the bodies to this obstacle reported that they negotiated it with as much skill as a master pilot.

Here ends Mr. Sadeur's story. It can be assumed in all likelihood that, having sailed soon after, he did not have time to write down the adventures of his return.

5. *Du Seigneur.*

Bibliography

The Text and Related Editions

The Present Edition

Translated from the original published at "Vannes" (Geneva). The Geneva edition consisted of 267 pp. in-12, plus the "Avis au Lecteur" and Table of Contents (i–xviii). This text is available in the 1922 Lachèvre edition, reprinted in 1968 (Geneva: Slatkine); in a facsimile edition introduced and annotated by Raymond Trousson (Geneva: Slatkine, 1981); and an edition introduced and annotated by Pierre Ronzeaud (Paris: Société des Textes Français Modernes/ Aux Amateurs de Livres, 1990).

Extant copies of the original edition (of 500 copies) are distributed as follows: *Europe* (7 copies): Bibliothèque Nationale; Bibliothèque de la Société de Géographie, Paris; Bibliothèque Municipale, Bordeaux; British Library (2 copies); University of Göttingen; University of Bologna. *United States* (7 copies): New York Public Library; Newberry Library; Michigan University; Clark Library, UCLA; Pattee Library, Pennsylvania State University; Columbia University. *Australasia* (6 copies): National Library of Australia (3 copies); State Library of New South Wales (2 copies); National Library of New Zealand. The number of extant copies is based on Kirsop (1980) and Ronzeaud (1990). There may be a copy in the Voltaire collection in St. Petersburg: cf. Ronzeaud (1982a, 54); Duchet (1971, 69); Storer (1945, 284). Kirsop notes two unverified holdings in the Hanover Landesbibliothek and Library of the Princes of Waldburg-Ziel, Baden-Würtemberg; and two lost during World War II (University of Munich and Bayerische Staatsbibliothek).

A Reedition of the Geneva Text

Identical except for a modified title: "Voyage / de la / Terre Australe / par Mr Sadeur / Avec ses Aventures / dans la découverte de ce pays jus- / ques icy inconnu & les particularités / du Sejour qu'il y fit durant trente- / cinq ans & son retour. A Lyon, / Chez Jean-Bapt. & Nicolas de Ville, / rüe Mercière, à la Science. / M.DC.XCV. [or M.DC.XCVI]." (Kirsop [1980]). 267 pp. in-12. 3 copies extant dated 1695 (John Carter Brown Library; Padua; Palermo), and 7 copies dated 1696 (Montpellier, Grenoble and Rouen Public Libraries; Milan; Bologna; Mitchell Library, Sydney). Total of verified extant copies of the Geneva text: 33.

The 1692 Version

Attributed conjecturally to Abbé François Raguenet: *Les Avantures de Jacques Sadeur / dans la découverte / et le voiage de la Terre Australe. / Contenant / Les Coûtumes et les Moeurs des Austra- / liens, leur Religion, leurs Exercises, / leurs Etudes, leurs Guerres, les Ani- / maux particuliers à ce Païs, et toutes / les Raretez curieuses qui s'y trouvent. / A Paris, / Chez Claude Barbin, au Palais, sur / le second Perron de la Sainte Chapelle. / M.DC.XCII / Avec Privilège du Roy.* 341 pp. in-16. The printing, by Laurent Rondet, was completed on 14 June 1692; Barbin's permission was for a period of eight years. Kirsop reports 35 extant copies: 13 in the United States, 11 in Australasia, 11 in Europe (1980). Leibacher-Ouvrard (1989, 221–23) notes an amusing anecdote pointing to Raguenet's editorship of the text, related 40 years later by Alain-

René Lesage. An unnamed publisher duped an author, Abbé---, into believing his work *Le Voyage des Terres Australes* had not sold, in order to pocket the profits (which indicates its popularity). When the abbé found out, he avenged himself by writing a novel totally inferior except for the first few pages; which the publisher eagerly snapped up. Since his work, *Siroës et Mirame, histoire persane,* was by Raguenet and published by Barbin (in 1693), the story points strongly to Raguenet's association with Foigny's work, and to the notoriety of the latter or of the austral topic in general at the time.

Reeditions of the 1692 Version

1693. A pirated version published in Holland, with the text further truncated and two different titles, the original one of 1692 and another: *Nouveau / voyage / de la / Terre Australe, / contenant / Les coûtumes et les Mœurs des Australiens, leur / Religion, leurs Exercices, Leurs Etudes, leurs / Guerres, les Animaux particuliers à ce pays / et toutes les Raretez curieuses qui s'y trou- / vent / Par Jacques Sadeur. / A Paris, chez Claude Barbin au Palais / M.DC.XCII. Avec Privilège du Roy.* 177p. pp. in-12. 24 extant copies signaled by Kirsop (1980), including one (Royal Library, Copenhagen) dated 1730, suggesting a possible second printing.

1705. A reedition of the 1692 text. Paris: by a consortium, La Compagnie des Libraires (Barbin's widow, C. Osmont, H. Charpentier, P. Ribou, P. Aubouyn or Auboüin, G. Cavelier, J. and M. Guignard, M. Clouzier, C. David, and J.-G. Nion). 341 pp. in-12. Kirsop locates 32 copies. It seems to have sold well and is the edition mentioned in the introduction, n. 22.

1732. Amsterdam: David Mortier, libraire à la Mappe-Monde. 330 pp. in-16. A reissue of the 1705 edition. 35 copies extant.

1786. Paris (extracts from the 1692 edition) in d'Argenson, *Bibliothèque Universelle des romans.*

1788. Amsterdam and Paris. The 1692 text, reproduced in vol. 24 of *Bibliothèque des Voyages Imaginaires . . . ,* edited by C. G. T. Garnier.

Translations

1693. The English translation of the 1692 version, with the title: *A New Discovery of Terra Incognita Australis, or the Southern World, by James Sadeur, A French Man who being cast there by a shipwrack, lived 35 years in that Country and Gives a particular Description of the Manners, Customs, Religion, Studies, and Wars, of those Southern People, and of some animals peculiar to that place: with several other Rarities. These Memoirs were thought so curious that they were keept secret in the closet of a late great Minister of State, and were never published now since his Death.* Translated from the French Copy. Printed at Paris, by Public Authority, April 8, 1693. Im-primateur Charles Hern; for John Dunton. In-12. 20 extant copies known. Dunton himself wrote fantastic voyages, such as *A Voyage Round the World: or, a Pocket Library*, 3 vols. London: for Richard Newcome, 1691. The first of these relates *The Rare Adventures of Don Kainophilus* {"lover of novelty"}, *From his Cradle to his 15th year, etc.*

1701. Dutch (from 1692 version): *Nieuwe reize na het Zuid-land behelzende de gewoontens en zeden der Zuidlanders . . . Door Jacques Sadeur* (New voyage to the Southland, with the customs and manners of the Southlanders . . . by Jacques Sadeur). Amsterdam: Willem de Coup. In-4. 12 copies known (3 in the Netherlands, 9 in Great Britain, the United States, and New Zealand).

1704. German (from 1692 version): *Sehr curiöse Reise-Beschreibung durch das neu-entdeckte Südland . . .* (Very curious description of travels through the newly-discovered Southland). Dresden: Johann Jacob Winklern, 1704. In-12. 6 copies known (3 in Germany).

1978. Italian (from 1676 version): *La terra australe . . . (etc.).* Edited with introduction by Maria Teresa Bovetti Pichetto. Naples: Guida, 1978.

Combined Editions

n.d. The 1692 text, published with *Nouvelle relation de la Gaspésie . . .* by a Franciscan missionary, Père Chrestien Le Clercq, as *Nouvelles relations de la Terre Australe et de la Gaspésie.* Paris: for

Amable Auroy, printed by Laurent Rondet. Kirsop (1980) located the work in the National Library of Australia.

1701. The Dutch translation of the same year is (in 7 of the 12 extant copies) combined with Vairasse's *History of the Sevarites* and with the journal of the *Nijptangh* (one of De Vlamingh's ships on his visit to Australia in 1696–1697), under the title *Beschryving van't onbekende Zuyd-land . . .* (Description of the unknown Southland). Amsterdam.

1793. The text of the 1788 Garnier edition was combined with a French translation of Fielding's *Julian the Apostate*, as *Julien l'Apostat, ou voyages dans l'autre monde; et les aventures de Jacques Sadeur, dans la découverte et le voyage de la Terre Australe.* Paris: chez Gay et Gide (. . .) et Belin. In-8.

Foigny's Other Works

La facilité et l'élégance des langues latine et française comprises en XCI leçons expliquées avec tant de clarté qu'une personne de jugement pourra se perfectionner en l'une et l'autre langue en un an et moins; de plus un abrégé de toutes les phrases françoises plus difficiles à expliquer en latin; avec un petit traité des poësies latine et francoise. 2 vol. (192, 136 pp.) Geneva: Jean Hermann Widerhold, 1673. In-8.

L'usage du jeu royal de la langue latine, Avec la Facilité et l'Elégance des Langues Latine et Françoise, Comprises en XCI Leçons, Le tout expliqué avec tant de clarté, qu'on pourra se perfectionner en l'une et l'autre Lange, en six ou sept mois. De plus, Un abrégé de toutes les phrases Françoises plus difficiles à rendre en Latin. Enfin Un petit Traitté des Poësies Latine et Françoise. Par Gabriel de Foigny. A Lyon, Chez la Véve de Benoit Coral Ruë Mercière à la Victoire, M.DC.LXXIV [1674]. 3 vol. (96, 192, 136 pp.). In-8.

La facilité et l'élégance des langues latine et françoise . . . Lyon, Chez la Veuve Coral et Th. Amaulry, 1674. In-12.

L'usage du jeu royal de la langue latine avec la facilité . . . Lyon, Chez la Veuve Coral et Th. Amaulry, n.d. In-12. No date according to Ronzeaud (1990, lxxxvii), although Lachèvre (1968, 165) signals an edition dated 1676.

Facilitas linguae gallicae et latinae . . . (Latin translation). Geneva: apud authorem, 1677. In-12 (Ronzeaud, 1990).

Les Pseaumes de Marot et de Bèze. "Charenton" (Geneva), 1674. This work, published by Gamonet, is not extant.

Le Grand Garantus. Geneva, 1674–1677. Almanach, not extant.

Expression de regrets causez par la mort de son Altesse Sérénissime monseigneur le prince Philippe, Landgrave de Hesse Cassel etc., son frère. Geneva, 1675. A funerary oration, 5 pp. In-4.

Secondary Sources

Adam, Antoine. 1962. *Histoire de la littérature française au XVIIe siècle.* Vol. 5. Paris.
———. 1964. *Les Libertins au XVIIe siècle.* Paris: Buchet-Chastel.
Adams, Percy G. 1962. *Travelers and Travel Liars.* Berkeley: Univ. of California Press.
———. 1982. *Travel Literature and the Evolution of the Novel.* Lexington: Univ. of Kentucky Press.
Africa, Christine E. 1979. *Utopias in France, 1616–1789.* Ann Arbor, Mich.: University Microfilms.
Alfonse, Jean. 1559. *Les Voyages avantureux de Jean Alfonse.* Poitiers: Jan Marnef.
Atkinson, Geoffroy. 1920. *The Extraordinary Voyage in French Literature before 1700.* New York: Columbia Univ. Press.
———. 1922. *The Extraordinary Voyage in French Literature from 1700–1720.* Paris: Champion.
———. 1924. *Les Relations de voyage du XVII siècle et l'évolution des idées.* Paris: Champion.
Bayle, Pierre. 1697. *Dictionnaire historique et critique,* 2:987 ff. ("Sadeur" article; cf. also "Adam" and "Salmacis"). Rotterdam: Reinier Leers.
Benrekassa, Georges. 1974. "Le statut du narrateur dans quelques textes dits utopiques." *Revue des Sciences Humaines* 39, no. 155: 378–95.

————. 1978. "Anthropologie, histoire et utopie: le cas des Aventures de Jacques Sadeur." *Modèles et moyens de la réflexion politique au XVIIIe siècle,* 2:78–108. Lille: Université de Lille III.

————. 1980. *Le concentrique et l'excentrique: marges des Lumières.* Paris: Payot.

————. 1985. "La Matière du langage: la linguistique utopique de Gabriel de Foigny." *La Linguistique fantastique.* Edited by S. Auroux, 150–65. Paris: Denoël.

Beretta Anguissola, Alberto. 1982. "Mostri e immaginario illuminista. *La Terre Australe connue* di Foigny." *Paragone.* Dec. 1982. 42–68.

Berneri, Marie-Louise. 1950. *Journey Through Utopia.* London: Routledge and Kegan Paul.

Bontekoe, Willem Ysbrantsz. 1929. *The Memorable Description of the East Indian Voyage, 1618–25.* Translated by C. B. Bodde-Hodgkinson and P. Geyl. New York: McBride.

Bourez, Marie-Thérèse. 1984. *"La Terre Australe connue* et *l'Histoire des Sévarambes* (1677) de Denis Veiras." *Le Voyage austral.* Edited by J. Chocheyras. Grenoble: E.L.L.U.G. (Université de Grenoble). 22–43.

Bovetti Pichetto, Maria Teresa. 1976. "Gabriel de Foigny, Utopista e Libertino." *Il Pensiero Politico.* 2–3:365–95.

Broc, Numa. 1975. *La Géographie des Philosophes.* Strasbourg: Université de Strasbourg.

Busson, Henri. 1948. *La Religion des classiques (1660–1685).* Paris: Presses Universitaires de France.

Campbell, Mary. 1988. *The Witness and the Other World: Exotic European Travel Writing, 400–1600.* Ithaca, N.Y.: Cornell Univ. Press.

Capetti, Alberto. 1981. "Les sauvages hermaphrodites de Foigny." *Studi di Letteratura Francese.* 7:100–115.

Chinard, Gilbert. 1913. *L'Amérique et le rêve exotique dans la littérature française au XVIIe et au XVIIe siècle.* Paris: Hachette. Reprint. Geneva: Slatkine, 1970.

Chupeau, Jacques. 1977. "Les récits de voyages aux lisières du roman." *Revue d'Histoire littéraire de la France.* 3–4:536–53.

Cioranescu, Alexandre. 1972. *L'avenir du passé. Utopie et littérature.* Paris: Gallimard.

Cornelius, Paul. 1965. *Language in Seventeenth and Eighteenth Century Imaginary Voyages.* Geneva: Droz.

Coulet, Henri. 1967. *Le Roman jusqu'à la Révolution.* 2 vols. Paris: Armand Colin. 1:280.

Cro, Stelio. 1990. *The Noble Savage: Allegory of Freedom.* Waterloo, Ont.: Wilfred Laurier Univ. Press.

Demoris, René. 1974. "L'utopie, Autre du roman: *La Terre Australe connue . . .* de G. de Foigny (1676)." *Revue des Sciences Humaines* 39, no. 155:397–409.

———. 1975. *Le Roman à la première personne.* Paris: Armand Colin.

Derrida, Jacques. 1976. *Of Grammatology.* Translated by G. C. Spivak. Baltimore: Johns Hopkins Univ. Press.

Descartes, René. 1971. *Philosophical Writings.* Edited and translated by E. Anscombe and P. Geach, introduction by A. Koyré. Indianapolis, Ind.: Bobs-Merrill.

Dubois, Claude-Gilbert. 1987. "L'Hermaphrodite." *Cahiers de Littérature du XVII siècle.* 9:11–27.

Elliott, Robert C. 1970. *The Shape of Utopia: Studies in a Literary Genre.* Chicago: Univ. of Chicago Press.

Fausett, David. 1988. *Amnioticon: histoire de l'utopie "australe."* Ph.D. diss., Ecole des Hautes Etudes en Sciences Sociales, Paris.

———. 1990. "Pour une histoire de l'imaginaire austral: de l'ailleurs fictif au territoire d'exploration." *Ailleurs imaginés.* Edited by J.-M. Racault. Paris: Didier (Cahiers CRLH-CIRAOI). 6:169–81.

———. 1993. *Writing the New World: Imaginary Voyages and Utopias of the Great Southern Land.* Syracuse: Syracuse Univ. Press.

Friedrich, Werner P. 1967a. "The Image of Australia in French Literature from the 17th to the 20th Centuries." *Mélanges . . . offerts à M. Brahmer.* Warsaw. 219–30.

———, ed. 1967b. *Australia in Western Imaginative Prose Writings, 1600–1960. An Anthology and History of Literature.* Chapel Hill: Univ. of North Carolina Press.

Garagnon, Jean. 1984. "*La Terre Australe connue* de Gabriel de Foigny: note sur le problème de l'authenticité de la seconde édition de 1692." *Dix-septième siècle* 142. 51–53.

Girsberger, Hans. 1924. "Der utopische Sozialismus des 18. Jahrhunderts in Frankreich und seiner philosophischen und materiellen Grundlagen." *Zürcher Volkswirtschaftliche Forschungen.* 1. Zürich: Saitzew.

Gove, Philip Babcock. 1941. *The Imaginary Voyage in Prose Fiction, 1700–1800.* New York: Columbia Univ. Press. 98–108.

Guicciardi, Jean-Pierre. 1980. "L'Hermaphrodite et le Prolétaire." *Le XVIIIème siècle: Représentations de la vie sexuelle. Revue du dix-huitième siècle* 12. 49–77.

Hazard, Paul. 1963. *The European Mind, 1680–1715.* Translated by J. L. May. New York: World Publishing.

Imbroscio, Carmelina, ed. 1986. *Requiem pour l'utopie? Tendances autodestructives du paradigme utopique.* Introduction by R. Trousson. Pisa: Goliardica; Paris: Nizet.

Kirsop, Wallace. 1980. "Gabriel de Foigny et sa *Terre Australe connue* (Genève, 1676)." *Cinq siècles d'imprimerie genevoise.* Edited by J.-D. Candaux and D. Lescaze. Geneva: Société d'Histoire et d'Archéologie. 341–65.

Knowlson, J. P. 1963. "The Imaginary Languages of Veiras, Foigny, and Tyssot." *Journal of the History of Ideas* (April–June, 1963): 269–78.

———. 1975. *Universal Language Schemes in England and France, 1600–1800.* Toronto: Univ. of Toronto Press.

Kuon, Peter. 1980. "L'Utopie politique: Foigny, Veiras, Fontenelle." Memoir, Romanisches Seminar, Universität Tübigen.

———. 1986. *Utopischer Entwurf und fiktionale Vermittlung: Studien zum Gattungswandel der literarischen Utopie zwischen Humanismus und Frühaufklärung.* Heidelberg: Carl Winter Universitätsverlag.

———. 1987. "L'Utopie entre 'mythe' et 'Lumières': la *Terre Australe connue* de Gabriel de Foigny et *l'Histoire des Sévarambes* de Denis Veiras." *Papers in French Seventeenth Century Literature* 14 (26): 253–72.

Lachèvre, Frédéric. 1968. *Les Successeurs de Cyrano de Bergerac.* Geneva: Slatkine. vol. 12. (ed. princ. Paris: Champion, 1922).

Lanson, Gustave. 1908. "Origines et premières manifestations de l'esprit philosophique dans la littérature française de 1675 à 1748." Paris: *Revue des Cours et Conférences* 16:11–15; 17:146–47.

Le Hérissé, A. 1911. *L'Ancien Royaume de Dahomey.* Paris.

Leibacher-Ouvrard, Lise. 1984. "L'Un et le double: hermaphrodisme et idéologie dans *La Terre Australe connue* (1676) de Gabriel de Foigny." *French Forum* 9:290–304.

―――. 1986. "Sauvages et utopies (1676–1715): l'exotisme-alibi." *French Literature Series* no. 13. 1–12.

―――. 1989. *Libertinage et utopies sous le règne de Louis XIV.* Geneva: Droz.

Lestringant, Frank. 1990. *Le Huguenot et le sauvage: l'Amérique et la controverse coloniale en France au temps des guerres de religion.* Paris: Aux Amateurs de Livres and Editions Klincksieck.

Lévi-Strauss, Claude. 1968. *Tristes Tropiques.* New York: Atheneum.

Lichtenberger, André. 1895. *Le Socialisme au dix-huitième siècle.* Paris: Alcan.

Linon, Sophy-Jenny. 1988. "L'Exotique dans les techniques d'écritures de deux récrits de voyages authentiques dans les Indes Orientales: *Relation d'un voyage des Indes Orientales,* Dellon (1685) et *Les Voyages aux Isles Dauphine et Mascarigne,* Dubois (1674)." *L'Exotisme.* Paris: Didier (Cahiers CRLH-CIRAOI). 5:89–99.

―――. 1990. "Contraintes et enjeux idéologiques d'une topographie imaginaire: les Terres Australes inconnues d'Etienne de Flacourt (1661) et de l'Abbé Jean Paulmier (1663)." *Ailleurs imaginés.* Edited by J.-M. Racault. Paris: Didier (Cahiers CRLH-CIRAOI). 7:159–68.

Marin, Louis. 1984. *Utopics: Spatial Plays.* Translated by R. Vollrath. Englewood Cliffs, N.J.: Humanities Press.

McIntyre, Kenneth Gordon. 1977. *The Secret Discovery of Australia: Portuguese Ventures 250 Years before Captain Cook.* Medindie, Australia: Souvenir Press.

Markham, Sir Clements, ed. 1904. *The Voyages of Pedro Fernandez de Queiros (1595–1606).* 2 vols. London: The Hakluyt Society. Vol. 2.

Minerva, Nadia. 1986. "L'Utopiste et le péché: a propos de quelques utopies de la 'Frühaufklärung'." In *Requiem pour l'utopie?,* ed. C. Imbroscio. 73–91.

Mühll, Emmanuel von der. 1938. *Denis Veiras et son Histoire des Sévarambes (1677–1679).* Paris: Droz.

Negley, Glen R., and J. Max Patrick. 1952. *The Quest for Utopia.* New York: Schuman. 400–19. (This work gives Patrick's translation of part of the 1676 "Notice to the Reader," and a short extract from the 1693 translation).

Nettlau, Max. 1897. *Bibliographie de l'anarchie: utopies littéraires.* Paris. Reprint. New York: Burt Franklin, 1968.

Patrick, J. Max. 1946. "A Consideration of De Foigny's *La Terre Australe connue.*" *PMLA* 61:739–51.

Pellandra, Carla. 1986. "Transparences trompeuses: les cosmogonies linguistiques de Foigny et de Veiras." *Requiem pour l'utopie?,* ed. C. Imbroscio. 55–71.

Pomeau, René. 1967. "Voyage et Lumièras dans la littérature française du XVIIIe siècle." *Studies on Voltaire and the Eighteenth Century* no. 57. 1269–89.

Pons, Etienne. 1932. "Les Langues imaginaires dans le voyage utopique." *Revue de littérature comparée* 12. 501–32.

Racault, Jean-Michel. 1991. *L'Utopie narrative en France et en Angleterre de l'âge classique aux Lumières (1675–1761): Etude de forme et signification.* Oxford: Voltaire Foundation.

Rihs, Charles. 1970. *Les Philosophes utopistes. Le mythe de la cité communautaire en France* au XVIIIe siècle. Paris: Marcel Rivière.

Ronzeaud, Pierre. 1978. "La Femme dans le roman utopique de la fin du XVIIe siècle." *Onze études sur la femme dans la littérature française du XVIIeme siècle.* Edited by W. Leiner. Tübingen: Narr; Paris: Place.

———. 1982a. *L'Utopie hermaphrodite: la Terre Australe connue de Gabriel de Foigny (1676).* Marseille: C.M.R.

———. 1982b. "Raison et déraison dans l'imaginaire utopique: *La Terre Australe connue* de Gabriel de Foigny." *Rivista di Letteratura Moderne e Comparate* 35. 141–57.

———. 1984. "Du détournement des cheminements culturels: le voyage utopique de Gabriel de Foigny." In *Voyages, récits et imaginaire.* Edited by B. Beugnot. Seattle: *Papers in French Seventeenth Century Literature.* 353–87.

———, ed. 1990. *La Terre Australe connue.* By G. de Foigny. Introduction by P. Ronzeaud. Paris: Aux Amateurs de Livres.

Rosenberg, Aubrey. 1971. "Digressions in Imaginary Voyages." In *The Varied Pattern: Studies in the 18th Century.* Edited by P. Hughes and D. Williams. Toronto: Hakkert.

————. 1972. *Tyssot de Patot and his Work (1655–1738).* The Hague: Martinus Nijhoff.

Rykwert, Joseph. 1988. *The idea of a Town: the Anthropology of Urban Form in Rome, Italy, and the Ancient World.* Cambridge, Mass.: MIT Press.

Spink, John S. 1960. *French Free Thought from Gassendi to Voltaire.* London: Athlone.

Storer, Mary Elizabeth. 1945a. "Abbé François Raguenet, Deist, Historian, Music and Art Critic." *Romanic Review* 36:283–96.

————. 1945b. "Bibliographical Observations on Foigny, Lahontan and Tyssot de Patot." *Modern Language Notes* 60:143–56.

Tieje, Arthur Jerrold. 1913. "Realism in Pre-Richardsonian Fiction." *PMLA* 28:213–52.

Trousson, Raymond. 1974. "Utopie et roman utopique." *Revue des Sciences Humaines* 39, no. 155:367–77.

————. 1975. *Voyages aux pays de nulle part: histoire littéraire de la pensée utopique.* Brussels: Editions de l'Université de Bruxelles.

————. 1977. "L'utopie en procès au siècle des Lumières." *Essays on the Age of Enlightenment in Honor of Ira O. Wade.* Geneva and Paris: Droz. 313–27.

————. 1978. "Eglise et religion en utopie." *Modèles et moyens de la réflexion politique au XVIIIe siècle.* Lille: Université de Lille III. 383–99.

Van Wijngaarden, Nicolaas. 1932. *Les Odyssées philosophiques en France entre 1616 et 1789.* Haarlem: Vijlbrief.

Vecchi, Paola. 1986. "L'Amour de soi et la mort en utopie." In *Requiem pour l'utopie?,* ed. C. Imbroscio. 35–53.

Vernière, Paul. 1954. *Spinoza et la pensée française avant la Révolution.* 2 vols. Paris: Presses Universitaires de France. vol. 1.

Watt, Ian. 1965. *The Rise of the Novel: Studies in Defoe, Richardson, and Fielding.* Harmondsworth: Penguin.

Winter, Michael. 1978. *Compendium Utopiarum.* Stuttgart: Metzler.

Yardeni, Miriam. 1980. Utopie et Révolte sous Louis XIV. Paris: Nizet.

The Southern Land, Known
was composed in 12 on 14 Garamond #3 on a Linotronic 300
by Partners Composition;
with display type in Caslon Openface
by Dix Type, Inc.;
printed by sheet-fed offset on 50-pound, acid-free Natural Hi Bulk
and Smyth-sewn and bound over binder's boards in ICG Arrestox B
with dust jackets printed in 2 colors
by Braun-Brumfield, Inc.;
designed by Mary Peterson Moore;
and published by
Syracuse University Press
Syracuse, New York 13244-5160

Utopianism and Communitarianism
Lyman Tower Sargent and Gregory Claeys, *Series Editors*

This series offers historical and contemporary analyses of utopian literature, communal studies, utopian social theory, broad themes such as the treatment of women in these traditions, and new editions of fictional works of lasting value for both a general and scholarly audience.

Other titles in the series include: